Praise for *Your 3 Best Super Powers*

"Sonia Choquette's life and work best testify to how well the 3 Super Powers truly work to create a magical life. I highly recommend this book."

— **Christiane Northrup**, *New York Times* best-selling author of *Goddesses Never Age*

"Sonia Choquette masterfully teaches us how to apply three simple universal principles that will change our lives for good: meditation, to free ourselves from our day-to-day distractions; imagination, to develop the capacity to envision and create more enriched lives; and intuition, to trust ourselves enough to effortlessly waltz into a new future. Your 3 Best Super Powers has not only changed the way I see the world, but has helped me create a better one."

— **Dr. Joe Dispenza**, *New York Times* best-selling author of *You Are the Placebo*

YOUR 3 BEST

SUPER POWERS

Meditation,
Imagination
& Intuition

SONIA CHOQUETTE

New York Times best-selling author

ALSO BY SONIA CHOQUETTE

Books/Oracle Cards

The Answer Is Simple . . . Love Yourself, Live Your Spirit!

The Answer Is Simple Oracle Cards

Ask Your Guides: Connecting to Your Divine Support System

Ask Your Guides Oracle Cards

Diary of a Psychic: Shattering the Myths

The Fool's Wisdom Oracle Cards

*Grace, Guidance, and Gifts: Sacred
Blessings to Light Your Way*

*The Intuitive Spark: Bringing Intuition Home
to Your Child, Your Family, and You*

*Soul Lessons and Soul Purpose:
A Channeled Guide to Why You Are Here*

Soul Lessons and Soul Purpose Oracle Cards

The Time Has Come . . . to Accept Your Intuitive Gifts!

Traveling at the Speed of Love

Trust Your Vibes at Work, and Let Them Work for You

Trust Your Vibes Oracle Cards

Trust Your Vibes: Secret Tools for Six-Sensory Living

Tune In: Let Your Intuition Guide You to Fulfillment and Flow

*Vitamins for the Soul: Daily Doses of Wisdom
for Personal Empowerment*

Walking Home: A Pilgrimage from Humbled to Healed

CD Programs

*Ask Your Guides: How to Connect with
Your Spiritual Support System (6-CD and 4-CD sets)*

*Attunement to Higher Vibrational Living,
with Mark Stanton Welch (4-CD set)*

*Meditations for Receiving Divine Guidance,
Support, and Healing (2-CD set)*

The Power of Your Spirit: Use It Now! (4-CD set)

*Trust Your Vibes at Work, and Let Them Work for You
(4-CD set)*

*Trust Your Vibes: Secret Tools for Six-Sensory Living
(6-CD set)*

All of the above are available at your local bookstore,
or may be ordered by visiting:

Hay House USA: www.hayhouse.com®
Hay House Australia: www.hayhouse.com.au
Hay House UK: www.hayhouse.co.uk
Hay House India: www.hayhouse.co.in

YOUR 3 BEST SUPER POWERS

Meditation, Imagination & Intuition

SONIA CHOQUETTE

HAY HOUSE, INC.
Carlsbad, California • New York City
London • Sydney • Johannesburg
Vancouver • New Delhi

Published and distributed in the United States by: Hay House, Inc.: www.hayhouse.com® • *Published and distributed in Australia by:* Hay House Australia Pty. Ltd.: www.hayhouse.com.au • *Published and distributed in the United Kingdom by:* Hay House UK, Ltd.: www.hayhouse.co.uk • *Published and distributed in the Republic of South Africa by:* Hay House SA (Pty), Ltd.: info@hayhouse.co.za • *Distributed in Canada by:* Raincoast Books: www.raincoast.com • *Published in India by:* Hay House Publishers India: www.hayhouse.co.in

Cover design: Amy Rose Grigoriou • *Interior design:* Bryn Starr Best

Cataloging-in-Publication Data is on file at the Library of Congress

Tradepaper ISBN: 978-1-4019-4456-8

10 9 8 7 6 5 4 3 2 1
1st edition, October 2016

Printed in the United States of America

*I would like to dedicate this book to David Bowie.
You are my great super hero now up in heaven.
Thank you for seeing me and making me feel
important all those years ago. The moment you did,
I realized how powerful and life-changing seeing
people really is. Inspired by you, I now dance
with people around the world.*

CONTENTS

INTRODUCTION

ARE YOU AWARE THAT ALL HUMANS are blessed with three incredible super powers that give you the ability to live with great peace of mind and tranquility, to create anything your heart desires, and to navigate through life in a guided and protected way?

Do you know that these three super powers can make you timeless, ageless, limitless, and full of vitality, if properly cultivated?

And that these super powers have the ability to guide you to make the best decisions, have the best timing, and flow with life in the best possible synchronistic way, adding magic and attracting joy along the way?

Do you know that your three best super powers can improve your health, ease your stress, eliminate your fears, and add to your abundance, while helping you fulfill a sense of purpose—all at the same time?

Yes, I know it is hard to believe that all of these suggestions are true, and yet they are. We humans all have access to three super powers that, if developed to their fullest capacity, give us the power to live the most magical and blessed of lives.

Better yet, it is not difficult to develop these super powers because they are innate in all of us. As spiritual beings, we have the power to live extraordinary lives by cultivating these three inborn qualities. And to do so is relaxing, easy, and readily attainable.

So just exactly what are these three super powers, you may wonder?

Meditation, imagination, and intuition. These are the three super powers that, when combined and used consistently, can determine the greatness and quality of your life's journey and keep you safe and secure every step of the way.

It is not difficult to develop these super powers because they are innate in all of us. As spiritual beings, we all possess the power to live extraordinary lives by cultivating these three inborn qualities. And to do so is relaxing, easy, and even fun.

Here's How They Work . . .

When we use our first super power—meditation—we control our response to our conscious thoughts, which gives us freedom and peace of mind. We detach from our monkey mind long enough to remember that we are not our intellect or our emotions, but rather spiritual beings on a human journey, endowed with the powers of thought and feeling, but not constrained by them. Meditation calms our minds, clears our heads, and relieves stressful thinking and feeling patterns. It gives us the space to refresh, revive, and rise above the mundane reactions of our ego mind in order to remember our true nature as divine and creative spirits, to remain in charge of our own destinies.

By cultivating our imagination, our second super power, we develop the capacity to envision and create enriched lives that are fulfilling and abundant in the ways that matter to us. Imagination is the paintbrush that colors the landscape of our lives. Our imagination determines who we choose to be, how we choose to live, and what we choose to do. Imagination is the force that defines our life's unfolding. Imagination is the energetic force behind all creativity. We cannot create what we cannot imagine, yet we always create what we do imagine. It drives human expression and experience on every level: mental, emotional, and physical.

When we exercise our third super power, our intuition, we avail ourselves of the grace of an inner guidance system that leads us to our hearts' desires and out of harm's way. Our intuition keeps us true to ourselves and in integrity with our authentic nature. As divine beings, we all have an inner guidance system designed to lead us to our fullest potential, our most authentic expression of self, and our highest good, while at the same time steering us away from what does not reflect our true nature, fulfill our sense of purpose, or keep us safely on our path. Intuition is the inborn compass that keeps us on course when we set sail for our greatest dreams, pointing out opportunities, while at the same time alerting us to danger and distraction if we drift from our true purpose.

When we develop these three super powers and put them into action in our lives, we become grounded, inspired, creative, abundant, and energized, flowing with a sense of peaceful purpose, and in harmony with the world around us.

These three super powers allow us to open our hearts, drop our defenses, wake up our spirits, and create our dreams. They ease our fears, eliminate our worries, give us the strength to face difficulties with grace, help us to recognize and seize opportunities, and show us the way to success every moment of the day.

These are the three super powers that all the successful and satisfied people I have guided and coached have possessed. It was their secret to success and I want it to be yours as well.

Your Super Powers Are Natural . . .

Fortunately, your three super powers are not super difficult to cultivate. They take desire, focus, and consistency more than complicated effort and a lot of time. That is because these super powers are natural to all of us.

We are naturally meditative creatures, as evidenced by the luxurious hours in which we daydreamed as children. We naturally imagine all the time, although our imaginings may not be so positive as of late. And we are all naturally intuitive, as well. We've just been coaxed away from listening to our intuition in most cases.

With a little awareness and some effort to wake up these super powers in you, you can expect to see a huge transformation in your life.

Perhaps you already engage one or two of these super powers. Perhaps you meditate already, for example. Or have a wild and wonderful imagination. Or maybe you are intuitive and listen to your sixth sense. If so, you have already seen the positive effect that a super power can have on your life.

Using any one or even two of these super powers does make a difference, maybe even a significant one. But what I have noticed, time and time again, is that when *all three* super powers are consistently engaged, a synergistic shift occurs and life starts to gain a super successful momentum that simply cannot be stopped. This momentum does not kick in until all three super powers are turned on full blast. They work together and build upon one another, like a perpetual motion machine of energy. One super power strengthens the next and the next until this wheel of energy takes off, attracting the best life has to offer directly to you.

When we are not in touch with any one of our three super powers, the results are less remarkable. The other two still make a positive difference, but not to the same degree as when all three are actively engaged on a consistent basis. When that happens—look out! Life takes a sharp turn for the better.

I have seen this to be true over years of working with my clients. I have also lived this truth for myself. And now I want it to be true for you as well.

WHAT YOU CAN EXPECT FROM THIS BOOK

This book is organized into three sections: Meditation, Imagination, and Intuition. Each is filled with anecdotes and easy-to-use tips and tools for how to awaken and expand the specific super power, and how to incorporate it into your everyday life.

There are two types of suggested activities to help you develop and unleash each super power. Some are one-time exercises, which I call "Jump Starts," because they are designed to jump-start the super power into action. These exercises take some planning and a little time, but are well worth the effort.

Others are tips about ways to quickly incorporate your super power into your daily flow. I call these "Boosters." These tips are not time-consuming, but rather offer easy ways to cultivate your super powers while going about your day without interrupting or changing your schedule in any way.

Developing these three super powers is not difficult. It just takes a few minutes a day, a willingness to try new things, and the mental flexibility to get behind your own success rather than stand in your own way.

Each super power, when developed, sets the stage for awakening and supporting the next. Meditation quiets the brain and disrupts habitual negative and stressful thinking patterns, thus freeing the imagination to focus on more inspiring, creative things. Imagination, once reawakened, opens the door to the more subtle energies of intuition and inner guidance. It is the bridge that allows us to make contact with our intuition and recognize the higher frequencies of our spiritual support systems, such as our spirit guides and angels. Most important of all, it allows us to feel the unconditional love and support of our Holy Mother-Father God, who is with us in every breath.

How to Use This Book

I encourage you to first read the book cover-to-cover just to see what it's all about. Then go back to the beginning and take your time. Read each section with an open mind and give all the techniques a try. That way you will be able to discover which ones work for you and which ones don't.

You don't have to use all the techniques all the time in order to harness your super powers. You only have to adopt one or two from each section and practice them daily, until they became a habit and develop into the super powerful abilities they can become. With daily practice, you will immediately begin to see changes and improvements in your life. They may be small at first, but as time goes on, their effects will snowball.

Some of the exercises in the sections on imagination and intuition later on in the book involve writing, so before you begin working with those sections, you will need a small notebook as well. Get one that is easy to carry and have with you at all times as you work with these two super powers. It will become a very important and powerful tool in its own right.

Having taught these three skills for more than 35 years, I have observed what works and what doesn't for many different types of people. In these pages I offer the best, simplest, easiest, most interesting, and most engaging tips and exercises that I have culled from decades of working with students from all types of backgrounds, all around the world. I guarantee that from among them you will find the combination that will wake up your super powers and put them to work right away.

THE GIFT THAT KEEPS ON GIVING

I was motivated to write this book for many reasons. Not only is it my greatest joy to empower others as thoroughly and quickly as possible, I also recognize that we are all connected as one human family. What affects you affects me, and vice versa, and we all affect one another all the time.

Therefore, the more empowered and fulfilled each of us is personally, the better the world we all share will be. The more quickly we find our own inner peace, the closer we will move to world peace. The more fulfilled and abundant our own personal lives are, the more generous we can be in creating fulfillment and abundance for other people.

The best part is that by developing your three best super powers, you add to the beauty, peace, creativity, and harmony of the universe. These three super powers are gifts to you that keep on giving to the world.

YOUR FIRST BEST SUPER POWER:
MEDITATION

OF THE THREE BEST SUPER POWERS we as humans can develop, I believe meditation is the most important, because not only does it empower us in its own right but it also lays the foundation for our other two super powers, imagination and intuition, to develop to their greatest potential.

We start with meditation for a number of reasons, the first being that our thoughts create our lives, for better or worse, so having control over our thoughts—or at least having some control over how much we allow our thoughts to influence us—can have a tremendous effect on our lives.

Life simply goes better when we are filled with positive, loving, accepting, compassionate, healing thoughts. Yet few people are in constant possession of such uplifting thoughts, and most find themselves instead distracted by all too many worrisome, stressful, self-doubting, critical, fearful, and isolating thoughts. If left unchecked, these negative thoughts will end up controlling and enslaving us, ultimately sickening us mind, body, and soul.

If practiced consistently over time, meditation frees us from the habit of allowing our thoughts to control us. Even better, with some types of meditation we even start to replace our harsh thoughts with kinder, more loving and

1

compassionate ones. When that happens, we begin to feel better, have more confidence, and enjoy our lives more.

WHAT IS MEDITATION?

Meditation is simply the daily practice of quieting the mind and relaxing. It doesn't stop us from thinking, but it helps relieve us from being possessed or even enslaved by our thoughts, and it eases our reactivity to the world, inside and out.

Meditation reminds us to breathe, which in itself is a great relief, especially for those of us who are often rushing around, trying to manage more than feels comfortable, and having difficulty with keeping up with demands we face. We may find ourselves in our ancient fight-or-flight mode, breathing shallowly, our hearts racing, and in a state of constant alertness, none of which is good for our health—mental or physical. If this is the case, meditation becomes our medication.

It reminds us that we are not the thoughts that race through our minds, so many of which are negative, fearful, or full of anxiety and dread. Meditation encourages us to step back and gently observe our thoughts and feelings as though they were no more than cars passing on the road. When we meditate, we learn to let them go by, rather than chasing after them. This creates distance and detachment from thoughts and feelings that leave us feeling stressed and insecure.

Meditation creates more open space in our heads, more room in our bodies. It allows us to breathe, to relax, to regroup, to calm down, to move from fight-or-flight reactivity to observation and objectivity, and to move toward having much more conscious responses. Meditation helps us make better choices in our lives.

Meditation softens our hearts, opens our minds, eases our stress, and gets the mental "tigers" off our tails that bully and push us around and leave us feeling defensive and under siege. It allows us to surrender to the loving caress of our Creator, Mother-Father God, every day. When meditating, we move outside of time and space and enter the realm of timelessness, the place where our divine spirit lives. And that is very powerful indeed.

My En"chant"ed Introduction to Meditation

My own introduction to meditation was through chanting meditation, which I learned from my first psychic development teacher, Charlie Goodman, when I was just a teenager.

Charlie told me he was going to teach me to meditate, then asked me to close my eyes and follow his example as he took in a big deep breath and then let out a booming "OOOMMM." It shocked me.

I instantly burst out laughing and couldn't stop. I wasn't prepared for this and it startled me. I continued to laugh out of nervousness. He totally ignored me as he kept on repeating the in-breath, followed by "OOOMMM" after "OOOMMM."

For five minutes, I laughed and he chanted, neither of us stopping on account of the other. But then something strange happened to me. I stopped laughing and tried it. I took in my own less-than-deep breath and let out a faint, insecure teenage "ooommm."

When my little "om" connected with his big "OM," I felt our joined vibration flow throughout my entire body. I loved the feeling. It calmed me down. It quieted my mind. And because of that I did it again and again. I was meditating. We continued for another 10 full minutes.

At first I only "om-ed" when I was in class with Charlie, but in a matter weeks I found myself doing it under my breath just before I went to sleep at night. It was relaxing. I was a sensitive kid, and it helped me let go of my teenage worries. And when I did, I slept better and had great dreams.

Soon, I found myself "om-ing" during the day, as well. I "om-ed" in my car on the way to school. I "om-ed" my way home. I "om-ed" in the bathtub. I "om-ed" while preparing dinner and while doing the dishes afterward, even bursting into a few rounds of "Om, Om on the Range."

I liked om-ing. It stopped me from thinking and worrying. It had a soothing effect on me and helped me feel grounded and present. It made everything so much easier. The longer I did it each time, the more calm and relaxed I became.

Thus I was introduced to my first super power and began my lifelong commitment to the power and joy of meditation.

MEDITATE ON THIS . . .
"OM" JUMP START

Maybe you are a little curious about "om-ing" yourself right now.

Go on and give it a try.

Make sure you are alone so you do not feel self-conscious.

Start by taking in a big, deep breath. But rather than gulp in the air, purse your lips and sip it in like drawing on a straw, for as long as you can, keeping your belly soft as you do.

When you reach your full lung capacity form your lips into a round O shape. Now, slowly allow the air to pass through your lips while you sound out a long *OOOOOO*, pushing the sound out from your belly until you almost reach the end of your breath. Then press your lips together and end with an *MMMMM* sound.

That's it.

You did it.

Now repeat this, only the next time try to relax your throat and allow the sound to rise from your belly and flow freely through your throat and jaw, like a foghorn.

Enjoy this experience. Don't be too serious or you won't feel the pleasure and benefit of doing this.

Continue, only this time keep your eyelids closed and bring your eyes to the center point of your forehead, to the place of your third eye, your intuitive inner eye.

Be sure to keep your shoulders relaxed. Pull the air into your belly and push out the sound *OOOOOOMMM* from your belly.

Repeat this at least 10 times, more if you can. Breathe in deeply between each *OM* and exhale slowly with each *OM*, not rushing to the end.

You may feel a little light-headed after this, so when you complete your last *OOOOOMMMMM* keep your eyes closed as you return to your normal breathing pattern, until you feel steady and grounded inside.

Then slowly rub your palms together and place them over your eyes. Tap gently on the third eye with both middle fingers, and then pull your palms to your lap.

Allow your eyes to open and drift to the floor and breathe.

On the next in-breath, bring your eyes to eye level and breathe.

Allow your eyes to travel to the space above you and breathe.

Finally, bring the edges of your lips up to your ears and smile and breathe in.

Hold it for a moment, then exhale and relax.

That's it.

You have just completed your first simple meditation practice.

If you enjoyed this, do it a few times every day.

Another Reason to Meditate

One of the best reasons to meditate is that it slows down your reactivity, and helps you make more empowered and mindful decisions. It keeps you from reacting too quickly or being too impulsive, which can lead you to make automatic and unproductive decisions, or express unhelpful behaviors. Instead, it gives you the space to calmly reflect and fully examine your options and your situation, and even access your intuition about what is best for you before you decide to act.

For example, my client Robert, a school counselor in a public high school in Michigan, struggled to keep his students grounded and feeling supported under very difficult conditions. On most days he went home feeling exhausted, overwhelmed, and as though he had fallen short when it came to helping his students as much as he had wanted to. Still, he managed to keep his spirits up—that is, until an ambitious new school principal showed up. Eager to improve the overall school ratings, she started monitoring all the teachers and counselors at the school, including Robert, and began to regularly criticize them all for not doing enough (according to her). She particularly seized upon Robert, accusing him of not volunteering enough or being a positive enough team member at school. She further accused him of having a bad attitude and being hard to communicate with, accusations that had never been leveled at him before and that he did not feel were justified.

Day after day, Robert began to feel more and more agitated and defensive under this ceaseless assault, and one day, after dealing with a particularly difficult situation between two students, he lost his temper and screamed at his principal to get off his back when she showed up at just the wrong moment with yet another negative piece of feedback.

Needless to say, that didn't go over well, and he was given a warning and told he needed to enroll in a communication improvement class in order to keep his job. Robert called me, beside himself. He felt outraged and picked on, was angry and scared, and didn't know what to do to turn the situation around, even though he knew he must. Clearly, he was not free to lash out as he had and needed to get a grip on his emotions in spite of the constant provocation and criticism he was now experiencing on top of the already incredibly stressful demands of his job.

I encouraged Robert to start meditating as a way to relieve some of his stress and reactivity. I made it clear that while meditation would by no means take the place of self-control, it would enhance his ability to exercise it.

Desperate, he agreed. He began slowly, using a four-breath meditation technique to help himself calm down, I encouraged him to remember to practice this daily and, in between meditation times, to use the same breathing technique a few times before he reacted to any stress he was facing.

Relieved to have something to grab on to, he happily agreed to give it a try. Several months later, he called to tell me that meditation was saving his job and quite possibly his life, as he was no longer so worked up that he thought he would have a heart attack at any moment.

He said that while the principal continued to be provocative, he learned from meditating not to react as quickly as he once did. He came to recognize that the principal's ambitions were what drove her criticisms and not to take the feedback she gave him as personally as he had before.

While he continued to intensely dislike the woman, he stopped allowing her to cause him to question his value at the school. Instead, he just listened when she critiqued him, and replied, "Okay. I'll do my best." At the end of their last monthly faculty meeting, to his shock, the principal commended him in front of the other teachers as an exemplary employee and thanked him for taking her feedback so well.

Of course, the other teachers now sneered at him, but he breathed through this as well. He knew he could never please them all, and besides, his job was to take care of the students to the best of his ability and that was all that mattered.

Over time, with continued meditation, he stopped overreacting, defending himself, lashing out, and feeling as angry as he once had, and made it through each day without feeling as though he was about to blow. He was so impressed with his results that he introduced a meditation program to the students at school, and many of them responded equally well to it. It calmed their hormonal swings and helped the kids stay more grounded and focused, which, for a teacher, was the best gift of all. With the help of meditation, he even said he thought he could make it another six years to retirement.

The super power of meditation can lift us out of our subjective reactive mind states and keep us more centered—no matter how others behave. The change you desire may not occur quickly or all at once, but with practice and consistency, it will come.

Here is the Four-Breath Meditation I shared with Robert.

FOUR-BREATH MEDITATION JUMP START

Start by finding a quiet place to sit without disturbance for 5 to 10 minutes.

Once settled, look around the room as you begin to take a few deep breaths.

Once you feel relaxed, place your thumb and your forefinger together, and as you exhale, allow your eyes to close.

With eyes closed, inhale to the count of four. Hold to the count of four. Then exhale to the count of four. Hold to the count of four. Repeat. Take your time as you inhale, hold, exhale, and hold, to the count of four.

As you do this, imagine the space behind your eyes relaxing. This can really help you enter a deeper calm.

Continue the practice 10 times, then slowly return to normal breathing and gently open your eyes.

Once you open your eyes, don't rush to get up. It is important to ease back into your surroundings. Taking a few more seconds will make a big difference in how you feel.

This entire process takes only a few minutes and calms your emotions and eases stress and anxiety beautifully.

LIVE IN THE NOW

When we meditate, we bring our focus out of the past and future and fully into the present moment, insuring that we don't miss out on our lives.

When I meditate, I am able to feel at peace right now. I feel happy and at ease and find I am not waiting for some future thing to occur before I can be content. I actually love my life, with all its facets, as it is.

Meditation keeps me from getting trapped in bitterness and resentment over losses I experienced in the past. It has helped me keep my faith and humor, and helped me to develop patience and acceptance of life.

The mind is usually fixated on the past or future, draining our energy and blocking us from experiencing life in the now. When our thoughts become overly focused on the past, we often become frustrated and feel agitated, even angry at the way life has unfolded at an earlier point in time. We get sucked into the emotional quicksand of the past and are powerless to maintain our footing in the present, not to mention move forward into the future.

When we are focused on the future, by contrast, we slip into anxiety and dread, as we feel vulnerable and uncertain about what we cannot control. In this preoccupied, fearful mind-set, we actually check out of our bodies and are neither here nor there.

Both past- and future-focused thinking rob us of good feelings and creative energy, and cut us off from our intuition and from the support of others. When our brains are so busy focusing on the future or rerunning the past, we miss the present moment altogether.

I found this to be especially true right after my divorce. At the time, I was struggling with feelings of anger, failure, resentment, and shame, and was especially fearful of the unknown, as I had been married since my early twenties. I felt like I had lost a piece of my identity.

Everything had changed. My finances were a disaster, my stress levels were through the roof, my emotions were shattered, and my mind didn't know what to do.

I no longer felt comfortable in any part of my life. I didn't feel comfortable in the home I had shared with my ex-husband. I didn't feel comfortable in the city in which we had lived together for over 30 years. I didn't feel comfortable doing the things we had done together as a couple. I vacillated between despair and anger, and found myself free-falling into extreme anxiety when I looked back at what I had lost, or ahead into the void, given my new state of being.

Meditation saved me. Every time I found myself on the slippery slope of misery that my thoughts of the past and future brought up, I simply sat down for 20 minutes and meditated, finding that it kept me grounded in the moment, a place I could manage and where I found relief.

The present moment is the only place in which we actually have the power to choose, to create, and to direct our life in the way we want to experience it right now. That is why meditating on a regular basis is such a super power.

It frees us from the limbo of past and future, and gives us back the life we are living right now. If practiced on a daily basis, it allows us to more fully experience and enjoy the present moment. It certainly has done that for me.

MEDITATE ON THIS . . .
BEING PRESENT BOOSTER

Take a minute and look up. Breathe in slowly through your nose, and then out through your nose. Do this two or three more times. Try not to rush. As you breathe, notice the sounds around you. Listen in as fully alert a state as possible. Notice your heartbeat. Is it beating regularly or is it beating quickly? Don't judge. Just notice as you continue to breathe slowly. Next, notice what is right in front of your eyes. As you breathe, allow your eyes to trace the shapes of the things you see. Then see each thing in its entirety.

For example, you may see a window in front of you. Mentally trace the outline of the window with your eyes, focusing on every last detail, as you breathe. When you are done, look at the window as a whole. Finish by quietly saying, "Window," as you look at it one last time.

Move on to another object and repeat this process. Do it four or five more times. Don't rush. Take your time. This entire practice will only take a minute or two at most, yet it is a powerful tool to refocus your attention on the present moment.

When you are finished, notice your inner state. Breathe and relax. Do not be surprised if your mind is calm and quiet and you feel peaceful and fully present.

If not, try it again in a while.

Don't force it. Just be curious and notice what it feels like to be fully present. Relax and breathe and carry on with what you are doing.

MEDITATION IMPROVES YOUR PHYSICAL HEALTH

I worked with a client named Lisa, who had had a terrible time with her weight since she was a teenager. By the time I met with her, she was overweight by 80 pounds, and no matter what diet she attempted, she never succeeded in losing more than a few pounds, which she quickly regained.

Demoralized, she admitted defeat to me in one of our sessions. I asked her if she knew how to meditate. She said she had tried it a few times, but never felt she got it right.

"But if I thought it would help," she said, "I'd be willing to try it again."

Not only was her weight emotionally draining her, but she was also diagnosed with diabetes now, which worried her to no end.

"I don't want my weight problem to kill me. I worry about my diabetes and my heart, and yet I have had no success in dieting. I don't know what to do, and I'm scared," she confessed.

I encouraged her to give meditation a try for a few months and leave the dieting alone for now. "Let's focus on calming your nervous system and getting you more grounded. We'll see what happens after that," I suggested.

Relieved that I wasn't giving her another diet to follow, she agreed.

She practiced a very simple breath meditation I taught her called "Breathing in the Holy Spirit." She gave it her all for the following three months, and then called me for a follow-up coaching session, very excited.

"You'll never believe it, Sonia. Without dieting I have actually lost ten pounds just by meditating," she gushed.

"How do you think that happened, Lisa?" I wondered.

"I know how," she answered without a moment's hesitation. "I eat when I'm anxious or nervous, which is often. But meditation has helped with that. I sit and breathe as you taught me, and my anxiety seems to have gone way down because of it. The urge to overeat passes if I allow myself the time to meditate instead.

"I don't do it every time," she confessed. "But even if I don't meditate, I am aware enough to eat less than I would before because I know I'm not really hungry, just stressed.

"Overall, it's helping me lose weight to meditate every day," she said.

"I'm even ready to try a new diet, or at least a different way of eating, now that I know how to relax a little more. I actually think I can turn myself around."

I was so happy to hear this news from Lisa. She was so optimistic and encouraged by the results she got with meditation that I felt she actually would turn her weight and life around now that she had accessed this super power to help her.

Lisa's experience with meditation worked for her because she was truly motivated to have it work. She approached it with an open mind and was generally consistent in her practice. And once she started losing weight, her motivation to continue only grew.

I'm convinced that meditation can help relieve just about every ailment in the body, if we make a real effort. Of course, this doesn't mean you shouldn't follow your doctor's orders when it comes to your health. You must. But meditation can support your healing, as well as help you cope with physical and psychological challenges, if you give it a chance.

It is no mystery why. When we meditate, we reduce anxiety and fear, which lowers our stress levels tremendously. And less stress on the body means improved health.

According to many studies, meditation is conducive to better sleep, better concentration, and deeper states of relaxation, and has also been shown to:

- Lower blood pressure
- Decrease heart rate
- Reduce the risk of heart disease
- Boost the immune system
- Ease insomnia
- Lower cholesterol levels
- Increase serotonin, which elevates our mood
- Ease chronic pain
- Increase vitality

It even helps increase the body's ability to physically heal from sickness and injury.

There is more. Meditation:

- Increases your power of concentration
- Lowers reactivity
- Relieves anxiety and depression

- Helps boost your ability to focus and learn
- Generally increases your overall feeling of happiness

Even if you're not suffering a physical or psychological ailment, meditation is good preventive medicine, just like eating a balanced diet and getting enough exercise and sleep. There's no downside and plenty of upside to giving it a try.

Meditate on This . . .

If you are suffering with a physical ailment, I am sure your stress levels are higher than normal right now.

While continuing to follow your doctor's orders to attend to the physical part of your healing, try adding the following meditation practice to augment your energetic healing regimen.

Breathing in the Holy Spirit Jump Start

Sit quietly and in a place where you won't be interrupted for several minutes.

Take a few deep breaths, breathing in through the nose and exhaling out through the mouth with eyes open.

Keep your focus soft and simply enjoy breathing in and out this way a few more times.

Next, as you exhale, allow your eyes to gently close and resume breathing in and out through the nose as you would normally.

Place one hand on your belly and the other on your chest as you continue to breathe, observing the rise and fall of your chest and the expansion and contraction of your belly with each breath.

With each inhale, gently say, "I breathe in the Holy Spirit," as you observe your chest and belly expanding with the air.

And with each exhale say, "I release what doesn't serve me," as you observe your chest and belly contract as the air leaves your body.

Repeat this slowly 20 times, or more if you have the time and inclination.

Take your time as you do this and try to make both inhale and exhale about the same length.

If your mind wanders during this time, don't worry about it. Treat your thoughts like cars passing by on the road. When you notice that your mind has wandered, see it as chasing a car, and gently draw it back toward you. Then simply return to your breath and start the cycle again.

Don't scold yourself for losing your focus. Think of your mind as a playful puppy, easily distracted. Your job is to train it, and as we all know, it takes great patience to train a puppy. Getting angry will only backfire. Take it easy and bring your mind *gently* back to your breath and mantra when it wanders, which it will.

Let yourself enjoy the experience. Keep it simple. Feel the power of the Holy Spirit giving you life and healing, restoring you to wholeness with each in-breath, and clearing, cleansing, and releasing everything from your mind and body that does not serve your wholeness and well-being as you exhale.

Say, "I breathe in the Holy Spirit," with your in-breath, drawing in this heavenly power to heal.

Say, "I breathe out all that does not serve me," with the out-breath, exhaling all toxins, stress, and upset that disturb your health and inner peace.

When you are finished, take a few more breaths and allow your mind to wander and do whatever it wants to do.

Then gently open your eyes and allow them to travel to the floor and breathe.

Keeping a soft focus, bring them up to eye level and breathe. Last, focus for a breath on the space above you and breathe. Then get up and stretch and be on with your day.

Continue to feel the presence of the Holy Spirit in your body, circulating with your breathing, every time you think of your health from now on.

DEALING WITH THE UNEXPECTED

Another reason I believe meditation is such a super power is that if you meditate regularly, you can confront unexpected, stressful situations in life with much greater ease and presence of mind than you might otherwise.

Earlier this year, I found myself in such an ungrounded and fearful place just after moving to Paris. I had rented what was advertised on Airbnb as a glamorous two-bedroom apartment in the area near Montmartre. Instead of a glamorous two-bedroom, I was met with a very basic one-bedroom apartment with a makeshift wall running down the middle of it. There was a large window, on the other side of which were dozens of very stinky, roosting, cooing pigeons. It was in a very sketchy neighborhood full of drunks and garbage strewn about. So much for glamour.

I dropped my bags at the door and looked outside. People were racing in droves to the Place de la République to protest the slaying of 11 people at the headquarters of the satirical magazine *Charlie Hebdo* days earlier. My head was swirling with thoughts of all the people I had just left behind in the U.S., who swore I was crazy for moving to Paris at this time. I looked around and wondered if they might have been right.

Rather than stare out the window in fear as the entire city swarmed to protest the recent terrorist attack, I decided I would head out and flow with the rest of Paris, adding my voice to the protest.

Walking back to the apartment about an hour and a half later, it suddenly hit me that I had left my life, my friends, my beautiful home, and all that I had devotedly worked toward building over the past 30 years. I was starting all over. I almost panicked as I looked around the freezing, gray, shell-shocked city, wondering what on earth I had been thinking. I had to fight every instinct to succumb to my ungrounded state of rising fear and sadness for all that I had just left behind.

I remembered to breathe and relax in my heart and belly as my thoughts wandered. Using my footsteps to keep count, I breathed in to the count of four, held it to the count of four, then breathed out to the count of four, and held it again before starting over. With each step and breath I uttered to myself, "I am calm. I am safe. I am calm. I am safe," all the way back to my new home.

By the time I arrived back at the apartment, I actually felt calm and safe. My earlier panic had vanished and was replaced with a fully present state of curiosity. *I can do this,* I thought to myself. *This is not bigger than me. It is just an unfamiliar experience, and I feel a bit uncomfortable. I can adjust and trust my guidance to be here. I am okay, and I am on a big adventure.*

My years of meditating served me well that day. Despite being very unhappy with the overadvertised apartment that I had committed myself to for the next three months, I managed to laugh a little and reminded myself that beauty is in the eye of the beholder. Maybe to my landlord this *was* a glamorous apartment. And to be fair, it was within a 10-minute walk to Montmartre.

Rather than freak out, I simply relaxed and let myself feel disappointed without allowing it to completely take over my state of mind. I was still upset, but I was no longer afraid. As I sat and breathed, I didn't fight a thing. "Accept and relax. Accept and relax," I told myself as I settled down deeper into meditation.

I allowed my breath to ground me. After a few breaths, I intuitively felt all would be okay, and as much I hoped that Paris would heal my broken heart, I was also there to be part of the positive energy the city needed to heal *its* broken heart. We were connected in that way.

Life will always bring unexpected, and often stressful, situations. That is a given. But you can be prepared to meet them in a grounded way if you train yourself to meditate daily. This will condition your mind to respond to the unexpected more calmly and objectively. It's a way to keep yourself from getting caught off guard and going into panic mode when the unexpected occurs. Instead, you can remain clearheaded and respond in a productive way rather than adding more flames to the fire you are faced with.

MEDITATE ON THIS ...
"I AM CALM" MEDITATION BOOSTER

When you find yourself meeting the unexpected, you too can remain grounded and calm using the same technique I used that first day in Paris. If time and circumstance allow, take five minutes and go for a walk around the block or, if that's not possible, just back and forth a few times across the floor. This helps release some of the adrenaline flooding your body, which might otherwise leave you feeling trapped and trigger even more stress.

As you walk, breathe in to the count of four steps. Hold to the count of four steps. Breathe out to the count of four steps. Hold again to the count of four steps. Repeat.

As you breathe in, say to yourself, "I am calm."

As you breathe out, say it again.

Breathe in, "I am calm."

Breathe out, "I am calm."

Continue until you feel calm. Five to ten minutes of this, if the time permits, should be enough to reset your panic button. Rather than being frightened, you should now be in a more grounded position where you can accept, think things through, and respond responsibly and effectively to the situation at hand. One or two turns around the block, or 10 times back and forth across a room, usually does it.

Once you do feel calm, then decide what to do. Not before.

MEDITATION PROTECTS YOUR SERENITY

When we meditate regularly, we become more and more aware of disturbances to our serenity and how to protect it.

Getting in the car to run a few errands one day last year before I moved, I mindlessly snapped on the radio. I was immediately assaulted by a frightening news report on NPR that yet another American health-care worker had become infected with the Ebola virus, and the U.S. stock market had plummeted as a result. Then it got worse. The announcer interviewed someone who said that unless something changed in six weeks or less in treating Ebola at the source in West Africa, the world would be overwhelmed with this deadly disease and we would all be sunk.

By the time I arrived at my first stop, only 10 minutes away, my heart was pounding through my chest. I was infected with the horrific anxiety virus that listening to national news spreads every time I tune in. As I pulled into a parking spot, I found myself anxiously wondering if my family, my savings, and I were safe, and if not, what on earth I could do to protect us.

I was just about to snap off the radio and regroup when the announcer said that despite this dreadful news, at this time the chances of getting Ebola in America were very slim, and that the market had made a bit of a recovery after dropping from the sky earlier. In other words, we were safe at this time.

I took a deep breath, feeling as though I had just dodged a bullet. What relieved me most were the words "at this time." They brought me back to reality and reminded me to be mindful of the moment. While my body was still drugged by the adrenaline that had flooded my veins, my mind was sobering up.

I looked out the window. It was a gorgeous fall day and a brilliant pageantry of red, yellow, and orange leaves danced through the trees. Sucked into the drama on the radio, I realized I hadn't noticed any of this on my drive over. In fact, I didn't recall seeing anything at all. My nervous system was relieved by the sweet sound of silence.

Wow, I thought, *I was in such a wonderful state of mind when I got into the car, and yet, only 10 minutes later, I feel really stressed out and anxious. Not good.*

Lesson learned.

Protect your serenity and your sense of personal power. Don't allow it to be hijacked by frightening news reports or other needless intrusions. Our spirits are sensitive, even if we are not aware of this fact. We crave and need calm, so it's up to us to create and protect it. Only the addictive mind thrives on chaos and overstimulation, and being immersed in it doesn't make us feel good or empowered in any way whatsoever. You have the power to say no to drama and psychic disturbance. The more you use this power, the better you will instantly feel. I promise.

Just for today, say no to all energetic intrusions that rob you of energy, confidence, peace of mind, and joy. Get clear about what those intrusions are so you will be prepared to rebuff them and not get caught off guard and ambushed.

Things that may intrude upon your peace and rob you of your serenity include:

- Watching the news
- Listening to gossip
- Adding to gossip
- Surfing the Internet

- Watching negative TV shows
- Answering phone calls from people who only want to complain or dump on you

If you really want to succeed in calming your mind, begin by consciously choosing more calming behaviors and setting up calming boundaries in your life.

Meditation doesn't guarantee that we won't lose our serenity, but it does help bring an awareness of it to mind so you will at least be able to recognize when you are tempted to let it be stolen away.

Meditate on This . . .
Room to Breathe Booster

Every time you face a disturbance to your spirit, take a breather: a one-minute meditation time-out. Close your eyes and feel the tension in your body. Then breathe in through your nose and exhale out through your mouth as though you are blowing out 10 birthday candles, and as you do, allow all the tension to flow out of your body. Envision a light in the very center of your heart opening and expanding in all six directions as you breathe, creating a clear and undisturbed space all around you. See this clear space expand above and below the area of your heart, to the front and back of your heart, and out to each side with each exhale. Breathe until the clear space extends beyond the edges of your body by 6 to 10 inches. This is your personal space, your "room to breathe." Repeat this three or four times, and then resume breathing normally.

Notice how much less urgent and stressful you feel after doing this and how much more centered and serene you feel in your mind and body. I love my "Room to Breathe" one-minute meditation. It is a very centering, self-protective meditation that guards you from psychic disturbance, whether coming from without or within.

MEDITATION STRETCHES TIME

When I meditate regularly, I flow with life rather than fight against it. One reason is that I feel less rushed and harried. I am not sure how this happens, but meditation seems to somehow stretch time. When I meditate, I get a whole lot more accomplished, while still finding time to relax and enjoy myself. This is the greatest gift meditation offers us, as time is our most precious commodity. We don't want to waste a minute of it, because once it is gone, it is gone forever.

I realized that worrying (which I do more of when I'm not meditating) takes up time and makes doing whatever I am doing more difficult to accomplish. Fighting against whatever I am doing makes progress very tedious, and time starts to get away from me. It becomes a vicious cycle.

With meditation, I find my mind relaxes into whatever I am doing and everything flows more or less smoothly. Looking back over my career, I marvel at how I found the time to write more than 20 books, consult with clients full-time, and travel around the world teaching workshops, and still have time to raise and enjoy my daughters, spend time with friends, and have a generally full life.

I know that meditation gave me the time, and what a gift it has been. If that is not a reason to meditate, I don't know what is.

PREPARING FOR MEDITATION

Now that you are (hopefully) receptive to the benefits of this great super power and have tried a few of the simple meditation techniques I have shared thus far, it is time to get serious about moving into a deeper, even more empowering meditation practice. Rather than using meditation reactively, as a way to deal with stressful situations, try now to begin to meditate proactively, adopting a daily practice of meditation so that you are prepared to approach every situation from a calm, centered position.

Meditating is a lot like baking a cake. If you want a satisfying outcome, it is important to have what you need on hand before you begin. Just as when baking a cake, it doesn't work if you have to stop midstream to run to the store for one of the ingredients, when meditating, it doesn't work if your phone is constantly buzzing with incoming texts. A little prep work beforehand goes a long way toward insuring a successful meditation experience.

MAKE A COMMITMENT

Making a serious commitment to meditate is the best and most important way to prepare for success. This doesn't mean simply *trying* to commit; it means putting two feet fully in, with no excuses. If you show up to meditate every day, it will super-charge your life. If you don't, it won't.

In working with my students, I can tell immediately if they are going to succeed in tapping in to this super power by how committed they are from the get-go. Those who say "I'll try" will most likely fail. Those who say "I'm going to do this" usually succeed.

It all lies in your willingness to commit and stick with it, no matter what. Those who decide they are going to give meditation a real go set up the energetic space in their lives to make it happen. Those who feebly say they will try, having made no room for it, usually quit in less than a week. And it is easy to see why. Life can be very demanding, and if you are highly sensitive, overly responsible, or conditioned to put everyone else's needs ahead of your own, it becomes doubly difficult to fit meditation in.

It's also difficult to meditate if you are easily distracted or overcommitted, tend to be lazy, quit on yourself, or give up too fast on things that don't bring you instant gratification. I can be all of the above at times, so I know how easy it is to let your meditation time fall by the wayside. And every time I do, I regret it.

That is why you must commit to meditating every day, for at least a few minutes, ideally first thing in the morning, no matter what. Without this commitment, you will likely fail. There are a few reasons why I recommend making a morning commitment. The first is that your mind is still a bit groggy, so you will have less thinking to struggle against. Also, it's a great way to start the day, as it leaves you feeling calm, grounded, and in a positive state of mind, which is conducive to having a good day.

Also, meditating first thing in the morning lends itself to success because most people are usually quiet or still sleeping in the early hours, so the overall energy in the atmosphere is calmer than later in the day. Mentally give yourself permission to use this time to simply relax and breathe without worry.

However, if you don't happen to be a morning person, and getting up a few minutes early is nearly impossible for you, just find the time that works for you and commit to fitting in your meditation time at some point before you go to sleep. In fact, just before you go to sleep may also be a good time, perhaps instead of watching the evening news or a dumb television show, for example. The key is to commit and do it. Period. Every day.

One way that may help you succeed is to think of meditation much as you would think of taking a daily vitamin or medication for your health, such as blood pressure or high cholesterol medicine. Morning or night, just do it, no matter how you feel about doing it.

Even now, after many years of meditating, if I don't meditate first thing in the morning, it's almost impossible to fit it in later. But I do—otherwise I feel it. My day doesn't go as well. I become more impatient and reactive. I neglect other things I need to do for myself. I feel more easily agitated and overwhelmed, and I run out of time. Like sliding down a slippery slope, not meditating is as detrimental to me as not eating. It is that important and central to my well-being, and I believe it will be for you as well.

THE BREAKFAST OF CHAMPIONS JUMP START

This is a beautiful morning meditation practice, as it fills you with the blessings, grace, and unconditional love of the Holy Mother-Father God and gives you the energy you need to meet the challenges of the day with ease. That is why I call it "The Breakfast of Champions."

Here's how:

Find a beautiful piece of music that you love, that moves your heart, and that lasts about 10 minutes. Classical music such as a selection from Vivaldi's "Four Seasons," Mozart, or Bach works beautifully, as these selections resonate with the heart and entrain it to beat at the same pace, as if in deep meditation. If you prefer, you can listen to what I listen to when "sourcing," or in other words, drawing from divine source to fill you with all you need each morning: the song "Devi Puja" by Krishna Das. It is essentially a prayerful call to the heavens for help and blessings.

Once you select your music (don't put it on just yet), set your intention, remember your motivation, and find a comfortable place where you can relax without interruption for the next 10 to 12 minutes.

Start by taking three deep breaths, in through the nose and out through the mouth. As you exhale, place your tongue on the roof of mouth, just behind your teeth, and force out all of the air from your lungs, pulling your belly in as you do, as though blowing out birthday candles on a cake. Putting your tongue on the roof your mouth this way calms and quiets your mind.

Inhale again, noticing how much more deeply you can breathe in this time.

Again, place your tongue on the roof of your mouth just behind your teeth and exhale fully, completely emptying your lungs as before.

Inhale once again, this time pulling the air clear into your solar plexus.

Exhale. Only this time, open your mouth, heart, and throat, and let out the sound *AAAHHHH*. Then relax.

Take in a few more relaxing breaths. As you do, imagine a beautiful white light expanding from the very center of your heart.

Begin to breathe normally, while visualizing the white light slowly expanding throughout your body in all six directions—above, below, in front, in back, and side to side—and into the space beyond.

Using your imagination, watch the light continue to open up the space inside you and beyond to the space around you.

Start your piece of music. You can listen to it with or without headphones, as long as your hands are free.

Gently allow your eyes to close.

Rubbing your palms together, gently pull them apart, and feel the energy flowing from palm to palm. Doing this activates your hand chakras and energy centers.

Once you feel the warmth flowing, your hand chakras are now open and ready to receive God's grace and love as the energy flows in.

Listening to the beautiful music, turn your palms upward and breathe in a deep, relaxing way, in and again out, through the nose.

Relax into the music and imagine that God is pouring endless and unconditional love for you into the center of your upturned palms.

As you continue to breathe, mentally observe as the beautiful energy travels up your arms and into your heart, then spills over and fills your entire body with grace, blessings, nurturing, and strength. Imagine that this loving energy is watering the seeds of your heart's desires, bringing them to life.

Imagine God's love, giving all you need for this to be the best day of your life.

Continue to breathe and receive until the music comes to an end.

Then, without rushing, with eyes still closed, gently rub your palms together and place them gently over your eyes. Breathe in.

As you exhale, bring your palms down to your lap and gently open your eyes, allowing them to travel to your lap or the floor beneath you. Breathe.

Without rushing, breathe in once again, bring your gaze to eye level, and gently look around the room.

Allow your eyes to travel to the space above you, taking in your surroundings. Take in another deep breath.

As you exhale, look ahead, and bring the edges of your lips up to your ears and hold it. Breathe and smile.

Stand up, stretch, and gently move into your day.

If The Breakfast of Champions is too much, or you are simply not a morning person, try this simpler Morning or Bedtime Meditation instead.

EASY MORNING OR BEDTIME MEDITATION JUMP START

Set your alarm clock or your smartphone for 3 to 20 minutes, depending on how long you want to meditate.

Sit in a comfortable position and take a look around the room. As you do, set your intention for this meditation.

Be clear about why this meditation is important to you today. Once you set your attention you are ready to begin.

With eyes open, start with several deep breaths, in through your nose and out through your mouth.

As you breathe, look around the room and focus on your immediate surroundings.

Allow your mind to start to unwind.

Now gently close your eyes.

Notice the difference that closing your eyes makes in how you feel.

Allow your mind to relax further with each deep relaxing breath you take.

Next, as if running a scanner over your body from head to toe, notice all the tension, stress, and discomfort in your body. Don't focus too much on any one thing as you do this. Simply notice how your body feels as you continue to breathe easily, in and out through the mouth.

Now return your focus to your breath.

Count each in breath and each out breath, starting at one and finishing at 10. Then repeat.

Thoughts will come and go. That is normal. Do not worry about this. The minute you notice that you've gotten lost in a thought, simply come back to your breath and begin again at one.

Continue to breathe and count each breath until the alarm goes off.

Once the alarm goes off, don't rush to open your eyes. Instead, gently rub your palms together and place them over your eyes.

Tap gently on your third eye with your middle finger of both hands to stimulate your third eye of intuition and creativity.

Bring your palms to your lap and breathe in as you allow your eyes to open and travel to the floor. Breathe out.

Next, breathe in and allow your eyes to focus at eye level. Breathe out.

Breathe in and allow your eyes to travel to the space above you, then breathe out.

Finally, take in a deep breath and bring the edges of your lips up to your ears and hold it for a second. Smile.

When you are ready, stand up, stretch, and continue with your day.

Take It a Minute at a Time

Now that you know how important commitment is to your success, you may hesitate. Wait a minute, you might think. How big does this commitment have to be? What if I don't like it? What if I hate it? What if I cannot do it? Then what?

All of these are reasonable concerns. In fact, I just met a woman here in Paris named Gwynne who seemed very interested in meditation, but said, "Honestly, Sonia, my mind is like a car on a race track. It takes off the minute I open my eyes in the morning. The idea of sitting quietly for twenty minutes seems like it would be torture to me. I cannot imagine being able to do that at all. So I guess I cannot meditate, can I?"

I told her that was not at all true. If you have a mind like that (and frankly, who doesn't?), you just have to build your meditation muscles a little at a time. That's all. Don't decide if you can successfully meditate before you give it a fair trial. Fully commit to the trial period, and then decide.

First, I suggest a trial period of 40 days in a row before deciding if it is working for you or not. This is the amount of time it usually takes to develop a new habit and the time it takes to feel results.

Second, make a reasonable commitment and do not overcommit to how long you meditate every day. For example, if you commit to one hour of meditation for the next 40 days, you won't likely make it to the weekend before you fail to show up because that commitment is too big. And not necessary.

Start the trial with a few short minutes every morning and build up your time commitment. If you fully commit to meditation for 40 days without interruption, even if for only a minute or two, you will experience its powerful healing effect. Guaranteed.

The key to success is patience and consistency.

Commitment Tip: If you have never meditated before, or have a mind that runs wild, begin with two minutes at first. Add another minute every three days as you go along. By the end of 40 days you will be successfully meditating for almost 10 to 15 minutes a day. And that is enough to reap meditation's wonderful benefits.

HAVE REALISTIC EXPECTATIONS

The next step in preparing to successfully meditate is to have realistic, grounded expectations of your practice before you begin.

When I began learning to play the piano (which is a wonderful form of meditation, by the way), I was very enthusiastic. Learning scales was easy, and I loved and looked forward to playing for at least 30 minutes a day. But after a few weeks, it was time to start learning to play simple songs and then more complicated ones. This didn't prove quite as easy for me as playing scales was. Inevitably, I would make mistake after mistake, and I became more and more frustrated with the experience. Soon, I began avoiding practicing, finding one excuse or another, until in a matter of weeks I was no longer playing the piano at all. I decided I was no good. The truth was that I was just impatient and my ego didn't like the basic repetitive steps of being a beginner. I was in such a hurry to master the piano that I did not want to slow down, settle in, and teach myself the basics that were necessary to move on.

I believe something similar happens to a lot of people when they start to meditate for the first time. So many people that I have worked with have come back to say, "I meditated just fine when I was in your class or workshop, but on my own, I couldn't sit still for even a few minutes before I was driven to distraction, so I just gave up." For them, meditating feels like sitting with ants in their pants, and each minute is an excruciating, long, exasperating fight with their runaway mind. They feel as though they are more stressed and upset than before they were meditating in the first place. No wonder they give up.

I understand their frustration. When beginning to meditate, the effort often doesn't feel good when it is supposed to. In fact, it either feels as though we aren't accomplishing anything or it feels as though we are trying to either wrestle a bear into a cage or catch a slippery fish, not succeeding at either. It's not surprising, then, especially in the western world of instant gratification, that meditation just doesn't seem, at first, to deliver what it promises. So we give up and walk away.

We like to feel as though we are masters, rather than beginners, and if we don't feel as if we are mastering something fast enough, irritation and ego take over and we quit. We have high expectations of meditation, but the initial experience falls far short of reaching those expectations. That is why it is very important, when developing this fantastic super power, to embrace a beginner's mind and not expect masterful results too quickly.

Expectations Tip: Keep your expectations simple.

- *Expect your mind to wander.*

- *Expect to become restless and antsy at times.*

- *Expect to not want to do it.*

- *Expect that you may not feel much at first.*

- *Expect that you may not feel much even after a while.*

- *Expect that you will still benefit even if you don't notice it right away.*

- *Expect that with time it will get easier and easier.*

- *Expect that your effort will pay off.*

- *Expect that this is a welcome, healing break and not a task to master.*

- *Expect to improve and go deeper and deeper into meditation more quickly if you stick with it.*

- *Expect that every little bit counts.*

FIND YOUR PERSONAL MEDITATION STYLE

Part of your preparation is finding the meditation practice that works for you. The good news is that there are many ways to meditate, and they all work. You don't have to sit in a half-lotus position with your eyes closed and your back ramrod straight—that is, unless you want to. You can choose the way you meditate—and change the way you mediate at any time—and it will continue to bring real benefit.

My own meditation style has changed often over the years, and still does. In the beginning I used chanting and simple breathing practices for meditation. Later, I began daily walking meditation. I've meditated while practicing yoga. Now I do all of these.

I generally meditate twice a day now: a "Breakfast of Champions" meditation in the morning, and chanting meditation for 20 minutes at night. If possible, I also add mindful walking (which I will talk about later in the chapter) in the afternoon. It's not that I am a meditation maniac. I do these because I really enjoy all these ways of meditating and they help me immensely, given the intensity of my work.

You may be wondering how I have the time for around an hour of mindfulness and meditation a day. I make the time. It is easier than you think. (Of course, it helps that I don't watch much TV.) I often weave my meditation into my daily routine. Sometimes I chant when I take a bath or clean the house or chop vegetables. Or I might do a walking meditation on the way to the grocery store. Meditating while doing a particularly unpleasant chore, like vacuuming, actually makes the time pass much more quickly and leaves me feeling energized rather than exhausted.

Any style of meditation, practiced for a few minutes a day, is enough to reap rewards if done consistently.

SAME PLACE, SAME TIME WORKS BEST

In the beginning, when training your mind to relax, it helps immensely to meditate at the same time, and if possible in the same place every day. This repetition clues the subconscious mind in that it is time to settle down and meditate.

When I was a kid in school, just after lunch, every single day, we were asked to lay our heads on our desks for 15 minutes and told it was time to relax. With the exception of a few hyperactive kids, we all laid our heads down and were all relaxed within a minute or two.

Little did I know at the time that we were meditating, but we were. Our minds were conditioned by the daily repetition of this routine that it was time to calm down and rejuvenate, and so we did. Even the hyperactive kids would settle down in time. It just took them a little while longer.

I am quite sure that if the daily naptime ritual had happened at random hours, rather than at the same time every day, we would have been far less successful at unwinding. The consistency was the reason for our success.

Consistency can be hard to maintain. I meditate every day, but I can assure you that at least two out of seven days a week I am not in the mood to do it, even after all these years. I may have gone to bed too late. I may have an appointment I need to rush off to. I may want to be on strike or blow it off. I simply ignore these resistant thoughts and, like the Nike ad says, I "Just do it." I have found, in the end, that it is far easier and less mental work overall to show up and meditate than not.

What time and place work best for you? Pick your own daily meditation routine and stick to it.

Same Place, Same Time Tip: Establish a preferred meditation routine before you begin. First, choose a time and place where you won't be disturbed. Second, close your computer, silence your cell phone, and minimize other potential distractions (for example, shut the window if there is noisy traffic outside). Third, sit comfortably on a couch, chair, cushion or, carpet. Fourth, begin.

MINDFULNESS

Once you've gotten the hang of quieting your mind during meditation, the next step is to maintain that state between meditation sessions—to become mindful. Mindfulness is the practice of being fully present to whatever you are doing rather than allowing yourself to be distracted or preoccupied with other things. It is the intention to be in charge of how you respond to life rather than allowing life to push and pull at you, scare you, or intimidate you.

For a few hours out of each day, several days a week, I work on coaching and counseling clients. While it is the love of my life, it can be draining on my mind and taxing to my body.

At the end of each day, it is important for me to go outside for a mindful walk to cut the cords with my clients and their lives, and get recentered in my energy and my life.

My mindful walks usually last around 20 to 30 minutes, and on these walks, through the beautiful streets of Paris, I give my full attention to the world around me. Walking mindfully involves holding my head up high to keep me present and aware. I look with great interest at all I see, paying attention to the shops that line the streets, the beautiful golden street lamps running along the Seine River, the dog owners who bear a striking resemblance to their pets, what people are wearing, and the flowers abloom in almost everyone's homes. By the end of my excursion I am rebalanced, relaxed, and ready for dinner. When you walk mindfully, a walk anywhere can be just as fabulous as the streets of Paris.

Pump the Brakes

Mindfulness takes attention, discipline, and practice, and can be incorporated into every part of your day if you just allow your mind to slow down a bit. Start by practicing being mindful in the morning. Be attentive and aware as you prepare your morning coffee or tea. Listen to birds chirping outside your window as the sun comes up. Notice the smell of the brewing coffee or toast in the toaster. Sit quietly and mindfully sip your cup of coffee or tea without feeling rushed for a full 5 to 10 minutes. Just relax, breathe, notice the world around you, and bask in the peace.

This sounds easy to do, but if you are like me and hit the ground running every morning, it may be difficult to allow yourself a full 10 minutes of mindful presence. If you have kids, this becomes even more difficult. In that case, get up 10 minutes earlier than usual so you can sneak in that mindful quiet before being present with them. If you have a dog you need to walk, walk your dog mindfully, without rushing or succumbing to distractions like your phone.

Mindfulness is not a practice that necessarily requires you to set aside dedicated time. Rather, it is the practice of giving your full attention to your everyday activities, rather than being preoccupied with other things at the same time. The key to mindfulness is not to do or accomplish less, but to be less distracted and rushed when doing whatever it is that you normally do. Once you get in the habit of being a little more mindful, day by day you will begin to feel more satisfied and peaceful in your life because you will actually be experiencing it rather than rushing too quickly past it.

Mindfulness Tip: Notice what causes you to feel upset or unhappy, as well as what causes you to feel joy, ease, and inner relaxation. Write down these things to anchor them clearly in your mind.

For example:

- *Watching the news upsets me.*

- *Arguing with my teenage daughter upsets me.*

- *Leaving late for work and arriving late upsets me.*

- *Talking about politics with my family upsets me.*

Reminding yourself of how these common interactions and behaviors don't bring peace or joy into your life makes it easier to catch and stop yourself when tempted to make such unhappy choices. First be aware. Then mindfully choose not to engage in these things. Stop, breathe, and do something different. Move on to the things you enjoy.

For example:

- *I enjoy a warm bath before bed.*

- *I enjoy quietly meditating in the morning.*

- *I enjoy giving hugs to the ones I love.*

- *I enjoy leaving early for work so I can take my time and ease into the day.*

Remind yourself of these fulfilling things daily—and do them. We fall so easily into habits of behavior and mind that make us suffer and cause us stress that we just plain forget or ignore what we enjoy. Mindfulness returns our attention to the things that bring us happiness and inner calm.

Mindful Walking Booster

Mindful walking is the practice of paying attention to your steps and the world around you as you walk instead of being swept up in your thoughts. It is a wonderful alternative to sitting meditation, and one I use at least four or five times a week in order to clear my mind and recalibrate after working with many clients during the day.

Here's how:

Keep your head up and focused on what is in front of you as you walk.

Notice the world around you.

If you stop to speak to someone, give him or her your full attention.

If you stop to look at something, give it your full attention.

If you hear something, such as birds singing, stop and enjoy their song fully.

Walk at a comfortable pace. Not too fast. Not too slow.

Appreciate every step you take.

Taking a mindful walk is a luxury for many people, or may seem like one. It's okay to keep the walk short. Even 10 or 15 minutes of mindful walking does wonders for your mind, body, and spirit.

A walk at the end of the workday may seem out of the question, especially if you have a family waiting for you at home. Yet there are still ways you can fit it in if it's important to you:

- Walk the dog just after getting home.

- Walk after dinner, while everyone is engaged in his or her evening routine.

- Invite your partner, or your kids, to join you and make it a family affair.

- Park your car and walk around the block before going in to work or in the house after work.

What matters most is that you allow yourself to give your full attention to the walk, and to everything and everyone you encounter. Enjoy your walking experience without feeling or being rushed. The point of mindful walking is to be present to what is right in front of you, and not thoughts of the past and future, allowing you to relax.

Two Minutes to Freedom Booster

If you are a hyper-vigilant or reactive person, or if you come from or find yourself in chaotic or unsettling circumstances, it can be particularly challenging to allow your mind to relax enough to be mindful. You may feel too anxious to relax because you are busy patrolling the borders of your life, feeling unsafe, or as though you have to always be on duty.

One way to free yourself from this hyper-vigilant state is to begin with a two-minute mindful break. That's right, a full two minutes to close your eyes, take a breath, and listen inward to your heartbeat. Nothing more.

Here's how:

Plan your two minutes in advance. It can be when you get up, after your morning shower, while sitting in your car before you go into work, or just before walking in the door to greet your family after work. It can even be in the restroom, if that is your only option. The key to success is to take your two minutes at approximately the same time every day. That way, your brain becomes conditioned and knows that, for those two minutes, you are free to relax, let go, and breathe, and it cooperates.

Ask others not to interrupt while you take two minutes for yourself. Better yet, choose the optimal moment when others are not around. If people are always around, they can become trained to respect your two minutes if you ask them. If you make this meditation part of your routine, even small children will get the message and cooperate.

Before settling in to your two minutes, take a moment to prepare. Turn your phone on silent and set your alarm for two minutes. Choose a gentle alarm for when your two minutes are up, and keep the volume low so as not to startle you.

Sit comfortably in a chair and look around the room. Doing this assures your mind that you are safe.

Frown, and then relax your brow to help relieve tension.

Open your mouth until you hear a click in your ears to relax your jaw and relieve more tension.

Start the timer on your phone and close your eyes, as you let out a gentle sigh.

For the next two minutes, just focus on your breathing. Don't worry if your mind fights back and starts bouncing around. Just repeat to yourself, "Safe to relax."

Place your tongue on the roof of your mouth and slowly breathe, while placing your hand on your diaphragm. Push your belly out as you breathe in, filling it with air. Then, pull your belly in as if to meet your back as you slowly exhale. This technique helps calm the brain. (You can practice this a few times before you begin.)

As you breathe, occasionally relax your brow and forehead again. This will ease the tension you hold in your furrowed brow.

Before you know it, two minutes will have passed and your alarm will sound. When it does, take a final breath in and gently open your eyes.

Take another breath or two before stretching and getting on with your day.

SITTING WITH GOD

One of my favorite ways to calm my mind and meditate is through the power of daily prayer. When I pray, I first center myself with my breath, focusing on how it enters and leaves my body, and especially on that pause between breaths. This, for me, is the moment when I connect with my holy and loving Divine Creator, the Holy Mother-Father God.

Sometimes, especially if I am weary, have given too much of myself, or feel lost, confused, or uninspired, I use this meditation as time to sit with God and bask in his/ her holy grace and replenish. I empty my heart and soul and find that the silence that follows is deeply healing. I never expect God to answer me. I feel in my heart that heaven hears and knows what is going on inside me and can bring healing and peace to all that disturbs my spirit. Try it yourself and see if it has the same effect on you.

MEDITATE ON THIS . . .
SIT WITH GOD JUMP START

When you enter this meditation, imagine you are a small child entering the arms of the most comforting and soothing embrace.

Ask God to help you remember who you are and reassure you that no matter what you think or feel at the moment, all is well.

As you breathe in and out, silently pour your heart out to God. Unload all that you worry about, all that concerns you, all that scares you, and all that you yearn for in your heart.

With each breath, surrender to God all your concerns and worries. With each breath, place more and more trust in God to take care of you.

Ask God to hear you and to help insure that your thoughts and emotions are moving on the path toward your highest good and highest potential for service to the planet.

Ask God to remove from you those thoughts and feelings that cause you to drift into darkness and do not serve your spirit.

When doing this type of prayerful meditation, relax and breathe, enjoying the pauses between breaths.

Sit quietly for a few more breaths or as long as you want once you've poured your heart out. Just relax and breathe and allow God to soothe you.

This is the place of contact with the Divine. It is the place where we meet God.

CONCLUSION

I hope you are now ready to begin a meditation practice of your own and begin to experience this tremendous super power in your own life. It is free. It is simple. And it is worth it.

Don't turn meditation into another burdensome task that you must learn to master, but rather consider daily meditation a place to find refuge, relief, acceptance, renewal, calm, and quiet, loving acceptance. It calms you down and keeps you present to what is happening right now. Meditation is a gift to yourself that will make every aspect of your life feel far more peaceful, grounded, and manageable.

General Tips for Successful Meditation:

- *Don't be in a hurry—transformation takes time.*
- *Meditate consistently every day at the same time.*
- *Don't chart your inner landscape day by day. The benefits show up slowly, over time.*
- *Know that life is precious and that meditation slows you down enough to experience it as precious.*
- *Persevere.*

With dedication to your practice, you will soon discover that it's nice to meditate. No matter how you feel going into it, you will feel great coming out of it. Soon you will not want to miss out on the great feeling meditation brings. Meditation will make whatever time you have left in your life fruitful and fulfilling. I promise.

Now that you have discovered the joy of meditation, you are ready to move on to activating Super Power #2: Imagination. Having started meditating, you are now more prepared than ever to rediscover this natural power and put it to work for you.

Meditation quiets the mind enough to interrupt our habitual (and often negative) thought patterns and creates the space to begin to imagine once again in wonderful, creative ways, just as you did when you were a child. The way you were designed to imagine.

YOUR SECOND BEST SUPER POWER:
IMAGINATION

OUR SECOND GREATEST SUPER POWER is that of imagination. Is it our magic, our mojo, our miraculous energy, and the force we use to create our lives. Our imagination determines how far we allow ourselves to go and how big we dare to dream. It is the incubator of our creativity and of our life.

We cannot create what we cannot imagine. Conversely, we always create what we do imagine. Therefore, taking charge of our imagination and directing it to create the life we really want is a tremendous super power.

Imagination shapes both the world we experience internally and the outer world we inhabit. When we imagine that life is beautiful, we experience a beautiful life. In fact, the Academy Award–winning film *Life Is Beautiful,* which follows a Jewish librarian and his son during the Holocaust, perfectly demonstrates what a tremendous super power imagination can be. In the film, the father and son use their imagination to protect them from the horrors of a concentration camp, and even go so far as to create a beautiful life in the worst of human conditions.

When we imagine, on the other hand, that life is the worst—that we are unloved, unsafe, and unwanted—then our inner life becomes a personal hell. Our imagined perceptions shape and influence how we respond to others; because of our negative inner state, we put up defenses, close our hearts, become reactive, and push others away, thus creating the very things we fearfully imagine to be true.

Our imagination is very powerful and is working to create our lived experience all the time, whether we know how to use it or not. That is why it is so important to take charge of this super power, so we can use it to create our own beautiful life and not our own personal hell.

IMAGINATION CREATES EVERYTHING AROUND US

Stop for just a moment and look around the room where you are now sitting and reading this book. Everything you see, from the chair you are sitting on to the floor underneath your feet to the lights in the room to the windows, the walls, the furniture, the lighting, the art-work—everything was first imagined by someone before it came to be.

Take a minute to study the details of the space you find yourself in at this very moment. Notice the bright colors and intricate patterns of the rug on the floor, the details in the carvings around the fireplace if you have one, the shape of the lamps, and even the lightbulbs in the lamps. All of these creations are the result of someone's marvelous, ingenious imagination fully expressed.

When I stop and look at the world around me, I cannot help but be incredibly impressed by the power of people's imaginations to create truly amazing things.

Someone imagined flying airplanes, and now we have ones that carry hundreds of people at a time across the globe. Someone imagined the Internet, and now almost anyone can connect to vast volumes of information and speak to the entire world with a push of a button on a phone or computer. Someone imagined a talking mouse, and now we have amazing amusement parks all over the world. Someone imagined flying to the moon, and now we are discovering potential life on Mars. Water purification systems. Organ transplants. Robotic limbs. Suspended bridges. Cars that fly. Virtual-reality headsets. Bionic ears. The list goes on and on. Each is the outcome of someone's active imagination making life better for thousands of other people.

All of these are just examples of the boundless power of imagination we humans possess. There is no limit to what we can create when we use our power to imagine it is possible.

The more we develop and use our super power of imagination, the more fulfilling and fantastic our own creations become, not only affecting the quality of our own lives but also empowering us to improve the lives of our fellow human beings.

MERRY CHRISTMAS, SANTA

I first discovered the super power of imagination when I was only 10 years old, during the Christmas season. One Saturday morning, while watching cartoons on TV as usual, a commercial came on for the local news. It said that a secret Santa would be driving around Denver, where I lived at the time, looking for signs in the windows of people's homes that said, "Merry Christmas, Santa." If Secret Santa drove by your house and saw your sign, he would bring you a *big* Christmas present.

That suggestion absolutely captured my imagination. I wanted nothing more at that moment than to have Secret Santa come visit me. I wanted that BIG present and decided I would have it. I immediately set to work to make the best sign possible for Santa to see in our front window.

I got out sheets of school paper and taped them together, making a huge sign so he wouldn't miss it. Then I got out my crayons and wrote out the letters as large as I could: MERRY CHRISTMAS, SANTA. Next, I colored in the letters and put glitter all around the edges to make them sparkle, giving my sign all the more punch. I spent hours on my project, singing Christmas songs as I worked and feeling happy the entire time, as I knew in my heart that Santa would see my sign and I would soon have my BIG present.

As a finishing touch I drew pictures of Christmas elves and reindeer and a picture of my entire family waving to Secret Santa with big smiles on our faces. It was a masterpiece.

As I worked, I imagined how shocked my family would be when Santa drove by and stopped in front of *our* house. And how curious our neighbors would be when they saw the great BIG present he was carrying up *our* front porch stairs. I imagined smiling at everyone as Santa delivered the goods.

I wondered how big our present would be, as they assured us on the commercial that it would be a BIG gift.

Maybe it would be a huge toboggan that we could take to the park. Maybe it would be a swimming pool. Or a new car for my parents. Or toys for all seven kids in my family. Or a pony. Who knew?

My older brother Anthony asked what I was doing at one point and I told him I was making a sign so that Secret Santa would see it as he drove by and leave us a present.

He laughed and made fun of me for thinking my sign would be seen, but I dismissed him outright. I absolutely felt—no, *knew*—in my heart that Santa would see it and I would win the prize. There was no question I would succeed.

Once I finished coloring and glittering, I taped the sign up in the front window of our house and announced to everyone at dinner that Santa would be arriving soon with a huge present for us, so they should be expecting him.

Everyone laughed and snickered at my audacity, but I ignored them.

"Mark my words," I said (an expression my mother used all the time), "Santa will come to our house and leave a big present. You'll see."

On Monday afternoon, as I walked in the door from school, my mom met me with a huge grin on her face.

"You'll never guess who came to visit just minutes after you left for school this morning," she said. "And found me in my pajamas with curlers in my hair as I opened the door."

My heart leaped. "Who?" I screamed, not daring to believe.

"Santa Claus," she answered, "with an entire TV crew right behind him, just as you told us would happen. Apparently, he saw your sign and stopped. The doorbell rang and I couldn't for the life of me imagine who might be here so early in the morning. I thought one of you kids had forgotten something so, without thinking, I opened the door even though I wasn't dressed.

"Imagine my surprise when, instead of seeing one of you kids, a TV camera flew into my face as Santa bounded up the front porch stairs yelling, 'HO HO HO! Merry Christmas!' Behind him were three elves carrying a big box, all wrapped up."

She was laughing as she told me the story, still shaking her head in disbelief.

"It was embarrassing to be on TV looking like I did," she said, still laughing, "but Santa and his elves didn't seem to mind. In fact, I think they rather enjoyed it, seeing as they laughed the entire time. And he left something for you. Go into the living room and see."

I ran to look. Sitting in the corner of living room was the biggest COLOR TV I had ever seen in my life! I couldn't believe it! My plan had worked!

Up until then, whenever we wanted to watch a show, our family had all gathered around a small black-and-white TV with rabbit-ear antennae that rarely fixed the fuzzy reception. We fought to find the best spot on the floor to sit in front of it, and I usually lost out to my brothers. Now we could all sit comfortably to watch our favorite shows. It was fantastic!

The rest of the family couldn't believe it either. It was our Christmas miracle.

That event left a deep and lasting impression on my life. I learned my lesson: If you can imagine something, and if you take heartfelt action to support your imagination, it will show up in your life.

From that moment on, I realized I could use my super power of imagination to actually attract and create the things I really wanted in life. If it worked once, it could work again—I was convinced.

As of today, many years later, I can honestly say that that event shaped my entire future. I learned that imagination is power and have used it to my advantage ever since. The sooner you believe in your own power of imagination, the sooner you can put this super power to work for yourself as well.

THE SKY IS THE LIMIT

The sky is the limit as far as your imagination is concerned, and once you harness this super power, your life will reflect your imagination like a mirror. When you imagine and *believe* in your imaginings, a magnetic force is released that begins to pull these energies into your life.

The good news is that it is never too late to tap into this amazing super power of yours. We are all born with amazing imaginations and use them to shape our lives without exception. As we grow up, however, and find ourselves needing to depend on powerful people around us, such as our parents, or to please powerful people, such as our teachers, we begin to lose touch with our imaginations and focus instead on keeping those powerful people happy with us. In most cases we no longer feel free to imagine what we want, giving ourselves over to how others see and often demand that we see the world and what is possible for us. By the time we are adults, we may only experience brief glimpses of our uninhibited imaginations, and we can't expect such momentary flashes to create much.

In order to truly harness the power of our imagination, we need to do more than merely glimpse our dreams from time to time. Instead we must fully, deeply, and steadily focus our imagination on what we truly feel and desire for a sustained period of time. When I wanted Santa to visit me, for example, I spent hours and hours and hours concentrating on what I wanted as I made my sign and fully immersed myself in my vision and the outcome I wanted. It was the intensity of my vision that made it come true. That is the kind of intensity and focus we need when it comes to imagining our dreams to fruition.

Sometimes what we imagine shows up right away, as it did for me with Secret Santa, and sometimes it takes a little longer, as it has in many of my other imaginings. No matter how long it takes to create or attract what you imagine, I assure you that whatever you hold in your imagination long enough, steadily enough, and with enough feeling and belief will *always* show up, good or bad.

I know this may sound like New Age nonsense, but believe me, there is nothing new or nonsensical about this super power. Creative geniuses, trailblazers, and revolutionaries of all stripes—artists, scientists, athletes, business, and political leaders—know that our imaginations endow us with the power of creation, and if we learn to use them correctly, we can bring almost anything we visualize into existence.

Picasso affirmed the power of imagination when he said, "Everything you can imagine is *real*."

George Bernard Shaw acknowledged this power when he wrote, "Imagination is the beginning of creation. You imagine what you desire, you will what you imagine, and at last you create what you will." He was right.

At 96 years old, Tao Porchon-Lynch is the world's oldest yoga teacher, as well as an energetic ballroom dancer. Tao imagines that she doesn't age. "I don't believe in aging," she says. "There is just too much to see and experience in this life and I don't want to miss any of it." In her imagination she is timeless. Her body agrees.

Then there is Sara Blakely. She imagined creating comfortable pantyhose to wear in hot weather in Florida because what was available made her miserable. She put her imagination to work and in time created the perfect solution, a comfortable and breathable undergarment. Despite being repeatedly turned down by numerous hosiery manufacturers, she never wavered in her belief in her own vision. She never *hoped* she would succeed. She imagined only that she *would* succeed. And boy, did she! She is now the billionaire owner of Spanx, her imagined undergarment dream come true.

Paralyzed from the neck down, Matthew Nagle was utterly dependent on others. After he had a silicon chip implanted in his brain, it took him only four days of visualizing success before he could move a computer cursor on a screen, open e-mail, play a computer game, and control a robotic arm, without any help from others. His super-powered imagination restored some of his freedom and transformed his life.

Almost everyone throughout history who has succeeded in anything, big or small, can credit the power of their imagination. Consciously or not, they worked it like a muscle every single day until it became so strong and conditioned that their entire mind and body moved solely in the direction of their intended outcome. Only when we make ourselves conscious of this power do we really begin to put it into practice and take fuller advantage of its potential. That is when life starts to become very exciting.

WAKE UP YOUR IMAGINATION JUMP START

Get out your small notebook and write down what it would feel like to live without limitations—physical, cultural, societal, emotional. Focus on at least three areas where you presently feel restrained in some way. Then list at least three things you would be able to do without those limitations. Now imagine doing them.

Example: If I were not limited by my claustrophobia, I would . . .

1. Go spelunking.

2. Learn how to scuba dive.

3. Ride the elevator to the top of the Empire State Building.

YOU ARE A GREAT CREATOR TOO!
JUMP START

The people I mentioned above have created some incredible things using the power of their imaginations. And now, it is time to recognize that you too have already used your imagination to create some great things.

On a separate piece of paper, and not in your notebook this time, make a list of all the things you have successfully imagined and created in your life thus far, such as:

- Meaningful work
- A family
- A great vacation
- A wonderful relationship
- Good health
- A beautiful home
- Good friends

- Meaningful community
- First prize in a contest
- A personal best in a sport
- A delicious cake

Take your time and list as many creations as possible, big and little, as far back as you can remember. As you reflect, recognize how well you imagined these successes before they came to be. You have already used your super power of imagination in so many ways!

Keep the list in a prominent place and make it your sport to keep adding to it by writing down what you have successfully created each day. It can be as simple as finding a parking space in a crowded shopping mall, or preparing a first-class home-cooked meal, or successfully completing a big project you have been working on for some time.

This exercise gets you in the habit of recognizing your super power of imagination in action. Don't let a day go by without adding to the list. Make it a family practice, inviting each member to share his or her best creation of the day at dinner, for example. After doing this for a month, I guarantee your life will completely transform from one of chance at success to one of guaranteed success.

Imagine the Best

Every morning before we went off to school, my mom would say, "Expect good things. And I expect to hear about them when you come home."

What a super-powered way to start the day! As a result of her command, not only did I expect good things, my eyes and ears were open for them at all times. In expecting good things, I set my intention to create and attract them. I became habituated to having positive expectations from life—seeing the glass half-full rather than half-empty. I never considered defeat. I imagined everything would work out in the end. If it didn't work out, it only meant that it wasn't the end quite yet.

Since then, I have spent my entire life imagining and expecting good things. And because of this, good things keep showing up. I imagined and expected my first book to get published despite everyone telling me it was nearly impossible. I imagined and expected to travel the world, although nearly everyone I knew told me it was too expensive, not to mention unrealistic. I have imagined and expected people I meet to be kind, open, and supportive, although many have warned me to be careful, stay close to home, and watch my back, especially following the repeated terrorist attacks in my adopted hometown of Paris. I pay attention, to be sure, but I still expect and encounter wonderful people in France and the world over. And I fully expect this to continue.

I expect doors to open. I expect miracles to happen. I expect love to prevail. And for me, these expectations are fulfilled in the most miraculous ways all the time. They can be for you too, if you are able to imagine it so.

Expectation is the hidden magic behind imagination. What you expect is usually what you get. If you expect positive things, they show up. If you expect awful things, they show up as well. The power of imagination does not discriminate.

SURPRISE!

Many years ago, shortly after my first book, *The Psychic Pathway*, was released, a small publishing company in Finland run by a very enthusiastic woman picked it up. She loved it so much that she invited me to fly over and teach a workshop in Helsinki.

Once I landed, she couldn't have been more helpful and accommodating. She really wanted me to enjoy my time there, as well as for the workshop to be a tremendous success. In service to both, she asked me how she could help and what I needed for my class.

I told her that all I needed was a good microphone and a good sound system to play some music because we were going to dance a little during the workshop.

When I mentioned dancing, she gasped. "Oh, Sonia," she said, "You must remember we are in Finland. People here are much too conservative to dance. I think you should forget that part of the workshop because the audience will not join you, and you and they will be uncomfortable because of this."

I just listened to her, nodding as she spoke, then decided to completely ignore her.

Instead, I said, "Well then, they can sit and watch me dance, because that is what I am going to do."

She conceded to my request but wasn't happy about it. Perhaps more than being concerned for me, she was worried for herself. She didn't want the workshop to be a flop, as she had invested a lot to bring me there, and my plans didn't reassure her of this outcome.

The next morning, the students entered the teaching room very quietly, and as they sat down, I had to admit that it was, indeed, one of the most subdued groups I have ever encountered in all my years of teaching. *Maybe my host was right. Maybe Finns really don't dance after all,* I mused as they quietly seated themselves before me. Judging from appearances, it looked as if it was going to require a lot to get them to move.

I decided to challenge myself. *I'm going to get these guys to dance, one way or another, and hopefully surprise us all.* To motivate both them and me, the first song I played was "I'm a Believer," by the Monkees, one of my all-time favorites.

To the shock and amazement of my host, and to my relief, a lot of people recognized the song and spontaneously joined in, starting to both sing and dance with me. At first they were tentative, but by the refrain, inhibitions went flying out the window. It was so liberating and fun that after a few minutes, some of the audience members even got up on their chairs and danced!

All of us had a fabulous time—except one. The only person in the room who didn't dance was my host. She looked on, shocked, and didn't move a muscle.

Later that day she conceded that perhaps it wasn't Finland that didn't dance. It was she who didn't dance. She wouldn't allow herself to let loose and have some fun, and projected that onto everyone else. Her imagination was too locked down to let go, so she believed that was the way it was with everyone.

"It's me who can't imagine dancing, Sonia. Not Finland," she said. "Oh my God, I really need to loosen up!"

I just hummed, "I'm a Believer!"

IMAGINE THIS . . .
IMAGINE THE BEST BOOSTER

For one day, try imagining the best of everything and everyone, no matter what you have experienced in the past. Speak and act toward others as though they were the most wonderful, beautiful, enjoyable people to be around—and say so. Stretch your imagination and fake it if you must. Remember, this is an experiment in using your imagination to create something new, so give it your best shot and see what happens.

LET IT ALL HANG OUT! JUMP START

When in a room alone, play the song "I'm a Believer" by the Monkees and sing along at the top of your lungs. Take it a step further and, while you're at it, dance like you are Elvis Presley live onstage. It's okay to use your hairbrush as your microphone. Come on, give it a go! You have nothing to lose and the super power of your imagination to regain.

YOU NEVER KNOW

One of my teachers once said to me years ago, "Never assume you know anyone completely. Your ideas about others are rarely accurate, so keep an open mind or you might miss something wonderful."

It has also been said, "You don't see others as how they are, but rather as how you are."

I had the occasion to witness firsthand the truth in both of those statements.

Many years ago, I met with a physician for an intuitive consultation in my apartment, where I was living and working at the time.

We had a great session, but just as he was preparing to leave, he sighed and said, "I wish my wife were more open-minded so she could explore her intuition with me, the way I am with you. She is so closed off to it that it's depressing. I cannot imagine talking with her about intuition or dreams or creativity or anything that is not concrete. It simply does not interest her at all. She is so shut down to this world that she would probably divorce me if she knew I was here."

Just then the doorbell rang, and when I answered the intercom to let my next client in, the doctor's face turned absolutely white.

"What's the matter?" I asked, surprised to see him suddenly look so shaken.

"Oh my God!" he gasped. "That's my wife at the door."

Panicked, he ran out the back door just as she knocked on the front.

The irony in all of this is that in his experience of his wife, what he said was likely true. In all probability, she was not open-minded, intuitive, or curious about such matters *when she was around him*. Not because she wasn't capable of being this way, but because his imagination didn't allow her to be this way.

Once we imagine people to be a certain way, that is usually how we treat them, and consequently that is the behavior we draw out of them. If we imagine them to be wonderful, for us they will be. If we imagine them to be sour grapes, then we will get vinegar. They simply reflect back to us the images of themselves that we project on them, which may not be at all who they truly are.

IMAGINE THIS . . .
AN INTERESTING EXPERIMENT JUMP START

Get together with one or two people you know really well.

On separate pieces of paper, list 10 things that best describe the other person or people.

At the same time, list 10 things that best describe you.

In both cases, it is important to be honest but kind so that you and your friends can trust each other and feel safe in this exercise. This is not a "gotcha" moment in which you get to criticize or be criticized. Instead, it is an opportunity to stretch your imagination to see beyond your subjective point of view.

When you are finished, have your friends read their descriptions of themselves to you. Then have them read their descriptions of you. You do the same.

Compare your descriptions of one another.

Do the descriptions match?

Does anything absolutely contradict?

Were there any surprises?

Might you be limited in how you see both others and yourself?

Were there any positive qualities either you or they mentioned that were overlooked?

Were there any specific differences in how you saw one another?

Were there any qualities either you or they saw that, once pointed out, you were able to see, whereas you didn't before?

The important thing here is not to agree or disagree with one another's perspectives, but rather to expand your own to include more than you normally see. For example, you may view a friend as being cautious, but he or she describes herself as adventurous. While this may not be your experience of this person, instead of refuting this, now is the time to say, "Wow. I never saw that in you before. Tell me where and how you are adventurous because I would love to know that side of you." Again, be aware of how you communicate. True interest comes across in your voice very differently than it does when you are being subtly challenging. Have fun with this exercise. It is an eye-opener if you engage in it with the right spirit.

Imagine This . . .
Daydream Believer Jump Start

Get out your small notebook and write or simply answer a few of the following prompts out loud. Spend 20 to 30 seconds on each one and try to visualize the experience with all of your senses. For example, what do you look like? What are you wearing? What do you hear around you? What smells are present? How does your skin feel? What are you looking at? Who might be looking at you? How do you feel? Are you smiling? Making any sounds? See your projection in living color, as if watching a movie. Or, if you are not a visual imaginer, experiment with other senses. With which of your senses do you imagine the most powerfully? Try a few now, and come back later and try a few more.

Imagine:

- Dancing under the stars.
- Being a rock star.
- Swinging on a trapeze.

- Flying an airplane.

- Fire walking.

- Doing what you really love.

- Being really in love.

- Loving being real.

- Having and using a super power.

AND IMAGINE THIS . . .
IMAGINATION BOOSTER

Here are some activities that can stimulate your imagination. Pick one and try it now. Pick another and try it later.

- Read children's books and fairy tales instead of the newspaper.

- Buy crayons or markers and paper and spend 15 minutes coloring.

- Watch children's cartoons instead of the news.

- Read books about people who have imagined and succeeded at doing great things in their chosen profession or vocation.

- Peruse websites of wonderful places around the world where you would love to someday visit.

- Look at architectural and design magazines to open up your imagination to beautiful ideas for your home.

Keep Going . . .
Working Your Imagination
a Little More Jump Start

Try the following visualization exercise to help strengthen your imagination muscles even more. If you have a smartphone, you can record the exercise as you work through it.

Take a few deep, relaxing breaths, in through the nose and out through the mouth.

Release the tension in your body as you exhale.

Now close your eyes and bring your attention to your heart.

Allow yourself to focus on one thing you would love to experience more than any other thing at this time in your life.

It can be anything you want. The sky is the limit.

Use all of your senses as you do this.

Now answer the following, out loud, while recording it on your phone:

What do you look like in your wonderful personal dream?

What are you wearing?

Where are you?

What do you smell?

What colors, shapes, and images do you see?

What is the sound track in your daydream?

What does your experience feel like on your fingertips?

What does it taste like?

Who else is in your experience?

What are you doing together?

What are others in your imaginary experience doing?

The minute your mind starts to limit or discourage you, remind yourself that it's a dream, and in your dreams there are no limits.

If it is difficult at first, don't be discouraged. Imagination is a muscle, and if you aren't accustomed to using it in this way it can be a little resistant at first.

The good news is that this super power does spring back to life quickly enough if given a chance and some encouragement.

WONDER POWER

Wonder is a great tool for strengthening the super power of imagination.

When we wonder, we open the front door to the imagination and walk right in.

Leonardo da Vinci asked his apprentices to wonder about 100 things a day as a way to expand and stretch their imaginations to greater and greater degrees of possibility and inspiration. I started doing this for myself and with my students many years ago and have found it to be a powerful imagination booster.

IMAGINE THIS . . .
I WONDER JUMP START

In your small notebook write down 100 things you wonder about. Don't stop writing until you are finished in one session.

You can wonder about anything, from "I wonder why the sky is blue" to "I wonder how yeast makes bread rise" or "I wonder what exactly happens day by day while the caterpillar is in the cocoon."

The key to successfully "wondering" is that you simply ponder questions without seeking or even wanting an answer. Just allow yourself to open up to the mysteries of life around you.

Wondering opens our mind and leads us to consider possibilities that we might not have ever considered before. It wakes up our imagination and gets us out of habitual, rigid, and even lazy patterns of thinking and seeing. Wondering stretches our imagination and helps us make direct contact with the world around us without the negative filters and assumptions that distort our view and severely limit our lives.

IMAGINE THIS . . .
CHANGE THE CONVERSATION BOOSTER

The next time you are out with friends for dinner, instead of talking about the same old things you usually talk about, invite them to work their imagination muscles with you. Bring up the following questions for discussion and let your imaginations run wild together. Before you dive into the questions, make sure everyone understands that this is an invitation to imagine the possible and not a time to be pessimistic or negative, as it will ruin the fun—and defeat the purpose.

- What inspires you most?
- What delights you the most?
- How wonderful can you imagine your life will be?

- What has been your best creation to date?
- How much positive energy can you comfortably receive?
- What is your heart's desire right now?
- What captures your imagination today?
- What do you wonder about?
- What new discovery have you made about someone you know well?

AND IMAGINE THIS . . .
GET A VISION JUMP START

Creating a vision board is a great way to sharpen your imagination super powers. This is an especially effective workout for your imagination if you have a difficult time imagining new things in your mind's eye. A vision board is a collage of photos, pictures cut from magazines, and inspiring words that express and reflect the things you would love to experience in your life, arranged on a large poster board and left in a prominent place so you can look at it every day.

Creating a vision board is fun, and especially so when you invite friends or family to join you in making ones of their own. In addition to images you can use glitter, markers, crayons, stickers, and anything else that inspires you to make it dazzle. The entire process is wholly one of imagination.

I create several a year, and every time I do, sooner or later the visions on my board miraculously show up in my life. It's amazing how life starts to subtly conspire for your success once you create a vision board, especially when you look at it every day after you create it.

Seeing it day after day not only attracts the possibility from the outside. You also begin to shift and change on the inside and suddenly discover ways to bring your imagined desire into reality as well.

Margot, a client who lives in Germany, very much wanted to attend my advanced teacher-training class in a small town near Chicago. The only problem was that she did not have the airfare to make it possible. Undeterred, she held a very clear picture in her mind of coming. Having attended a workshop of mine in the same town a few years earlier, and being familiar with its quaint atmosphere, she envisioned herself looking at the holiday decorations around town and enjoying the smells of hot chocolate and cider that are so prevalent there at that time of year. She saw herself laughing with the other students and felt how wonderful it would be to learn new skills to bring back to her students in Hamburg. She saw herself in the classroom with me and never doubted for a moment that she would be there. She didn't know how this would come to pass, so she simply trusted her vision and kept on dreaming to the point where she was planning on it. Two weeks before the class was to meet and still with no means to buy the ticket, she found herself sitting at her desk working when quite spontaneously she got the urge to stop what she was doing and open her desk drawers and clean them out.

It was unlike her, and actually quite a distraction, to stop what she was doing and begin this new task, but she couldn't help herself. Fifteen minutes into the project, she pulled an old book out of the back of the drawer and out fell 1,000 Euros, which she had apparently put there some time earlier and forgotten about. It was just enough money to cover the round-trip airfare from Hamburg to Chicago. She laughed with delight and thanked God and her angels for making her dream trip come true, having known it would happen all along.

IMAGINE THIS . . .
JUST FOR FUN JUMP START

Create a vision board for an ideal vacation.
You will need:

- A fairly large poster board
- Glue and glue sticks
- A stack of travel, design, architecture, and fashion magazines
- Some music to listen to
- Photos of you and those you want to travel with
- A friend or two who wants to create a vision board with you

(Having several people gather at the same time to make a vision board amplifies the power of the board to help manifest the vision that it represents.)

Before you begin, set your intention to create a wonderful experience with a short prayer, such as:

"Holy Mother-Father God,
Please bless me in my creation and
fulfill my heart's desire in all ways.
Please allow all heavenly helpers to support
me in manifesting this dream.

Behold my vision and even improve upon it
to create this or better.
Thank you in advance for hearing and
answering my prayer.
Amen."

Now set to the fun work of decorating your poster board with all the images, words, and phrases that represent your ideal vacation. Do not worry about *how* this is going to happen. Just focus on the "what" and the "where" of your dream vacation and let the "how" be a surprise.

As you work, imagine yourself in the scene, having the time of your life. If it's a ski vacation, feel the cold wind on your cheeks as you fly down the mountain under a crystal blue mountain sky. Imagine how it would feel to maneuver around the moguls and swoop down the mountain, laughing out loud with glee as you do. Visualize sipping hot chocolate by the huge fireplace in the ski lodge as you watch soft snowflakes dance around outside the windows while you look out onto the mountain. Imagine melting snow dripping from your boots onto the floor as you warm your toes by the fire, relaxing after the most exhilarating fun of hours of skiing.

If yours is a vacation in Paris, imagine the sound of French accordion music wafting in your ears, or better yet, put on the music of Édith Piaf to set the mood. Envision yourself strolling down the Champs-Élysées or taking a boat ride down the Seine on a warm summer evening. Imagine sipping a delicious café au lait on the terrace of a French café while snacking on cheese and baguettes, watching people stroll by arm in arm, laughing as they go. Imagine yourself strolling across one of the famous Parisian bridges under the golden glow of ornate streetlights, taking "selfie" photos with the Eiffel Tower in the background, surrounded by lovers who pause to kiss and then skip off hand in hand. Now imagine strolling across the bridge with a lover of your own, a kiss of your own, and a skip of your own.

Maybe you would rather have the most delicious beach vacation on some exotic island. Imagine swimming in the warm blue waters surrounded by dolphins, or surfing the waves, then relaxing on the white sand beach under a big sun umbrella, gazing out at the rolling ocean waves. Imagine sitting on the beach watching the most gorgeous sunrise or sunset as the waves splash gently on your toes, children squealing in the background as they fill their buckets with sand to make their sand castles. Imagine the mystical sounds of tropical music playing in the background as you are served the most refreshing fresh fruit drink by a smiling attendant.

You get the idea. Or at least I hope you do. Putting together a vision board involves all of your senses. As you work, let your imagination come alive. Let yourself get lost in the experience for the pure fun of it.

Play music that inspires the feeling of being on vacation as you work. Sing along to your favorite songs as you put your vision board together.

When it is finished, prominently display your vision board somewhere where you will see it every day. Stop and look at it for a moment or two whenever you pass by and fully expect what it depicts to happen.

Then pack your bags and get ready to go. Believe me, you will.

(Of course, you can create a vision board for whatever you want—it doesn't have to be for a vacation. Just allow your imagination to run wild and have fun.)

Believing Eyes

Many of my clients and students over the years have told me that it is very difficult for them to imagine positive things in their lives. They have said that their lives have been so disappointing, so traumatic, so painful that they can't imagine anything different from what they have experienced so far.

I understand how they feel. There have definitely been times when my life has been so difficult, so painful, and so challenging that I have felt too defeated to imagine positive or uplifting things ahead for myself. For example, when I broke my knee kickboxing after separating from my husband, I worried that I would not be able to make a pilgrimage that I desperately wanted to go on. After eight weeks of hobbling around on crutches, barely able to put my full weight comfortably on my knee when walking up stairs, walking over 500 miles and through two mountain ranges seemed like a dream that couldn't possibly come true. Instead of imagining my success, I could only imagine all the impediments to it.

Yet I did know that in order to create that experience, I would have to be able to imagine it as possible first. So when confronted by these daunting obstacles, I knew it was time to ask for help and support with my imagination.

This is when I summoned what I call my "believing eyes."

The need to have "believing eyes" was first pointed out to me, years ago, by my dear friend Julia Cameron, author of *The Artist's Way.*

Julia suggests that when we are trying to create something new, better, and wonderful, yet find ourselves filled with doubt and fear, we seek out generous and loving friends who will uphold, reflect, protect, and believe in our dreams for us until we start to believe in them ourselves.

She actually did this for me herself when I first wanted to write and publish a book but doubted that it was possible. Julia had come to me as a client for intuitive guidance. Right after our consultation, she surprised me by intuitively tuning in to my yearning to be a writer and asking me about "my book."

Not expecting this, I admitted that it was my secret heart's desire to write about developing intuition and creating your dreams. But, I told her, I had never written before and had little confidence I could do it now.

I sheepishly pulled out from the closet a feeble attempt that I had previously made the mistake of sharing with another client, who was an editor. Filled with the hope of successfully accomplishing my dream, I had asked the editor to have a look at it, hoping for some words of encouragement. Instead, she'd returned it with a note asking me if English was my first language.

Her comment embarrassed me to no end and destroyed my confidence as a writer. I shoved the draft into the closet and decided right then and there that I would never embarrass myself again by trying to write a book. I then put it out of my mind.

That is, until that moment when Julia brought it up.

She said the editor didn't know what she was talking about and suggested that I share my book with her, because she could hardly wait to read it. She also suggested I write to her every day telling her a little more about living an intuitively guided life. Since she lived in Taos, New Mexico, at the time, she suggested that I fax my letters to her.

She was so warm and encouraging that, despite my reservations, I agreed to do as she asked. Every day thereafter, for several months, I wrote and then faxed her an essay on how to develop your intuitive abilities.

She eagerly awaited my faxes and faxed me backed a few hours after she received them with variations on the same response, essentially: "This is so exciting, Sonia. I am learning so much. Please tell me more. I cannot wait to receive your next fax."

Her enthusiasm and support fueled my confidence, and soon it became my greatest joy to send her my daily essay to read.

After three months, Julia faxed back and said, "I believe you have just written a book, Sonia." Then she helped me organize my essays into what became my first published book, and a dream come true, *The Psychic Pathway.*

My heart's desire came about with the help of someone who believed wholeheartedly in me. Without her "believing eyes," I am sure I would never have found the confidence to write that or any book ever.

With her help, I came to believe in myself. Thanks to Julia I realized that we don't need to struggle with our limiting imaginations and beliefs or be held back by them. Instead, we can break free by asking others to believe for us, with us, and in us until we can start to believe in ourselves. Their "believing eyes" act as training wheels for our imaginations.

Over the years I have studied the difference between those who have succeeded in achieving their dreams and those who haven't. In almost every case, not only did the person who succeeded tap into the super power of imagination, but he or she also had at least one pair of "believing eyes" in their corner. It reminds me over and over again that we need support and need to allow ourselves the ability to comfortably ask for and receive it if we are to succeed in tapping into this great super power of ours.

(And, by the way, with the help of my two daughters, who served as my believing eyes for the pilgrimage, I did go on my pilgrimage two months later, and made it all the way to the end. I even wrote about my experience in my book *Walking Home: A Pilgrimage from Humbled to Healed.*)

FINDING "BELIEVING EYES"

After hearing this story, some of my students have said to me, "You're just lucky, Sonia. You had a friend like Julia to believe in you. I don't have anyone like that in my life."

It may appear to be luck that I happened upon someone who served as my "believing eyes," but I don't attribute it to luck at all. It was God's grace, for sure, for which I am grateful. But it also came about because before Julia offered to be my "believing eyes," I was already doing that for her when she consulted me.

It works that way. The more you believe in others and lift them up, the more they will do the same for you. It's natural.

Sadly, in my practice over the years, I have noticed how very few people seem willing to freely champion others in this way. It is sad to see how rare it can be to witness people showing genuine and generous support for one another.

More often I witness people discouraging others rather than encouraging them. It happens for a lot of reasons. They become anxious, jealous, and competitive, or just fear being left behind, so they unconsciously hold others back to protect their own insecurities.

The ones who are willing to encourage others, however, are true earth angels. Those whose hearts are open and whose spirits generously and freely uplift others have tapped into their super power of imagination to jump-start the more limited imaginations of those whom they help. Like charging a dead battery, people who lend their power of imagination and belief to others who are struggling feel the energy and bring their own imaginations back to life.

Such people understand that there is no "them" in this world. There is only "us." We are all one, connected in spirit, and when one among us succeeds and is happy, we all benefit in the end.

What about You?

Are you someone's "believing eyes"? Do you encourage others to imagine and believe in their dreams? Do you believe with them? Do you assure them that all will come to pass as they desire if they keep at it? Do you believe for them when they are discouraged or doubtful?

When someone says, for example, "One day I'd like to have my own business," do you encourage his or her dream? Do you say, "What a great creation. I know you will succeed, and when you do, I'll be your first paying customer. I'll bring all my friends there as well"? Or do you say, "Good luck with that. Most businesses fail in the first year."

When you hear someone say, "I'd love to fall in love again," do you respond, "I am confident that the right person is on his or her way to your heart. It's only a matter of time before you are swept off your feet"? Or do you say, "I hate to break it to you, but at your age all the good ones are taken."

Do you act as "believing eyes" for your friends, or do you have what I call "stink eye," the negative eye that sees only doom and gloom and failure?

I don't know if you have noticed, but I notice that stingy people have stingy imaginations. Generous people have generous imaginations. Being generous of spirit by believing in others costs no money and little time, and quickly engages your imagination in a wonderful way.

The great thing about being another's "believing eyes" is that your own imagination grows along with your generous spirit and you start to believe in your own dreams as well.

IMAGINE THIS . . .
BECOME SOMEONE'S "BELIEVING EYES" FOR A DAY BOOSTER

Ask someone you care about what his or her heart's desire is.

When they share it, tell them that you believe in their dream and will continue to do so until they realize it.

If they shut you down or say, "It's only a dream," tell them that dreams come true, and you will believe in theirs for them until it does.

Afterward, notice how you feel.

Being someone's "believing eyes" is a gift you give yourself. The more you dream for and with others, and want the best for others, the more your own imagination grows and expands, while inviting others to do the same for you. Like a boomerang, the more you support others' dreams, the more others and the Universe will support yours.

The Power of Belief

Some people have told me that imagining is not "realistic," as they have "responsibilities" and cannot indulge in fantasies. This only shows that they have lost touch with their super power of imagination.

I caution you against being "realistic." What it really means is, "I am afraid of being disappointed."

People who don't want to risk being let down let themselves down first, before they even try to imagine something wonderful. Such people are in the habit of giving up before even trying to succeed and blame lack of opportunity on "reality" instead of their limited imaginations.

People who feel this way also tend to generalize their feelings as everyone's feelings as a way to justify their self-abandonment.

Just today, I spoke with a client named Laura who was afraid to leave her unfulfilling job and look for another one because she worried that she would not find another job, or worse, would end up in a job she truly hated. She didn't believe there were more fulfilling jobs out there, even though she hadn't looked at all.

Instead of looking, she said, "People everywhere are struggling financially, so I'd better be realistic and stay put in my job, even though I can't stand it."

She wasn't being realistic. She was being fatalistic and making herself miserable because of it. She had options, she just didn't care to explore them. She ignored her power of imagination and settled for guaranteed misery instead.

What most people call *realistic* is really a failure of imagination.

My client Evelyn desperately needed to sell her house. Her daughter had just had twins, one of whom was born with a serious heart defect. Evelyn needed to help her daughter out with the exorbitant medical costs as well as help care for her grandchildren. It only made sense to Evelyn that she sell her house and move nearer to her daughter as fast as she could.

When we spoke she was frantic. "I have to get to Maryland to help my daughter as soon as I can, and I'm afraid I won't be able to help her if I don't sell my house now. The market is down everywhere and my Realtor just told me it might be months before I could expect to attract a buyer. Realistically, I am stuck with my house and won't be able to move on as I need to. This is just terrible."

I told her that she didn't know what was and wasn't selling, and not to be so "realistic" that she closed the door to her desire and threw away the key.

I suggested she wake up her imagination by saying, every day, at least 10 times, out loud: "I am so excited that I sold my house, and for the full asking price at that." And to feel it was true when she said it.

Evelyn argued with me at first. I reminded her that she had nothing to lose, so why not give it a try? Upon my insistence she eventually, but very reluctantly, agreed. She thought I was nuts for suggesting such a crazy notion.

"Fake it until you make it" was my response. "Just try it as an experiment and see what happens. You don't have to believe me. Just test the theory."

"Okay, I will." She laughed. "Why not?"

She called me two months later. An unexpected buyer had shown up from another state to be near her aging mother and bought her house for full price, cash on the spot, because it was only two blocks away from where her mother lived. It seemed the buyer had the same motivation to help family as Evelyn did, so their connection seemed almost uncanny.

"It's unbelievable," Evelyn gushed. "No one can believe this happened—I can hardly believe it myself!"

I laughed and said, "I can."

FEAR AND WORRY

For a lot of people, what has usurped our super power of imagination is the super undoing of fear and worry. They're like the ugly stepsisters of imagination who moved in and now take all the fun and joy out of our lives. Fear and worry hold our imaginations hostage and wield a threatening dark power of their own.

If you don't think this is true, just reflect on how much fear and worry have laid claim to your imagination. Even if the things you fear and worry about do not come to pass, they might as well, because they can take up so much space in your mind that there is little room to experience or notice anything else.

Mark Twain noticed this when he said, "I have been through some terrible things in my life, some of which actually happened."

Think of the things you fear and worry about.

How much space do these things take up in your head?

How much energy do you give these thoughts every day?

How much time do these anxieties consume?

How much effort does it take to try and manage your life when fear and worry have taken over?

Simply notice. Then breathe and try the following exercise.

IMAGINE THIS . . .
EMPTYING THE GARBAGE JUMP START

This is one of my favorite tools for clearing away fear and worry and allowing your imagination to recalibrate to a higher, more creative vibration. Use it as often as you need to. It only takes a few minutes at most.

Sit in a comfortable chair and take a few deep breaths. Next, out loud, name something you are afraid of, such as, "I am afraid I won't be able to pay my bills."

Then breathe in and pick one thing in the physical world right in front of you, such as the window or the door. Look at it, focusing on as much detail as you possibly can. Then name it out loud: "I see the door." Then breathe again.

Next, imagine you have just taken that fear or worry out of your imagination and placed it in the garbage. Breathe out.

Then name another thing out loud that you fear or worry about. For example, "I am afraid I won't be loved and will be alone in life."

Again, take in a deep breath and name something in front of you out loud: "I see the wood floor under my feet."

Focus on it in as much detail as possible.

Then imagine placing that fear or worry in the garbage. Breathe out.

Do this over and over until you can no longer name anything you are afraid of or worry about.

Next, close your eyes and imagine taking the garbage out just as the garbage collector is driving up to collect it. Hand the garbage off to the garbage collector and watch the truck driving off.

Notice how quiet your mind is now that it is emptied of these fears and worries and refocused on the present moment.

Open your eyes and again notice and name something right in front of you. This anchors you even more fully in the present moment, free of the fear and worry that you were holding on to.

Take in a breath and say out loud, "All is well in this moment and that is all that matters." Breathe out.

Stand up and stretch and enjoy the lighter feeling that comes with having emptied the garbage.

Do this every day for a month. It only takes a minute or two and will free your imagination to work in powerful and supportive ways instead of against you.

Mark My Words

Your words have power, and using them to express your highest potential instead of your worst fears puts your imagination to work for you.

When I was growing up, my mom used to often say, "Mark my words, it will happen."

We did mark her words, and what she said usually did happen. We weren't surprised. We expected it.

I shared this with a client of mine and she took it to heart. She was part of a sales team competing in a contest to win a brand-new red Mustang. She said, "Mark my words, Sonia. I am going to win that car."

She not only imagined it possible, she counted on it—and said so, every day of the contest. Guess what? She did win, and even wrote a book to tell about it.

The reason words have such power is that they reveal what you imagine and believe.

Take it further and make up songs that affirm your desired outcomes. Singing something over and over imprints the subconscious mind and gets it on board.

I had a friend who sang, "The lottery win is mine. The lottery win is mine. Hi ho, the derry-o, the lottery win is mine."

He won at least once a month doing this, albeit small sums.

He said he was happy with that.

He combined all the tools of imagination, word, repetition, and belief, and had a great time with his lottery hobby.

FAVORITE AFFIRMATIONS BOOSTER

Here are some of my favorite affirmations. Pick one and repeat it to yourself 25 times today. Tomorrow, pick another.

- God loves me and I love me.
- I am blessed, beautiful, and bountiful.
- I walk in God's grace and in the company of angels.
- I am easily lovable and greatly loved.
- All is well and I am grateful for my blessings.
- No worries. All is well.
- My needs are never too much and will be met in perfect ways.
- I am free of the past and present to all blessings in my life now or coming my way.

- I am grateful for my life.
- I will have what I need when I need it.
- I love myself.

DO YOU IMAGINE THE WORST?

I often find people use their imagination in reverse. Rather than imagine beautiful things, they imagine the worst. They see the world through the lens of negative expectation and this negative expectation becomes a self-fulfilling prophecy. It is the "See, I told you that would happen" use of imagination.

As Jesus said, "And their fears shall come upon them."

I was again reminded of just how quickly imagining the worst can attract the same a few summers ago, when a friend of mine, Mara, came to Paris to visit me.

She hadn't been to Paris in a while. Just before she came she had been warned several times (including once by me when she arrived, I am sorry to say) to watch for pickpockets in Paris in the summer, as they are particularly predatory at that time of year and very good at what they do.

She asked about pickpockets several times, wanting to be sure she avoided them, but since most of the time we were together, I told her not to worry as I knew what and whom to watch out for.

One morning, she decided to take her son to the Eiffel Tower and asked if I wanted to go with her. I declined, as I had been there dozens of times, so she and her son went on their own.

They left at 8 in the morning and returned by 10. Excited to hear of their adventure, I was greeted instead with her story of how, five minutes after she sent her son up to the top to see the view, she was pickpocketed by the best Paris has to offer.

"I knew it was going to happen," she said. "I kept feeling it. It was inevitable."

Knowing the power of imagination, I agreed.

She had imagined it happening so well that she attracted the pickpockets like flies to the light.

Fortunately, the damage done was minimal and did not ruin her trip, but sadly, it did dampen her affection for Paris a little.

POWER THROUGH CONSISTENCY

Some people have challenged my insistence that imagination is one of our top three super powers by asking, "Are you saying that everything that we imagine will come true?"

Fortunately, it does not. If it did, we would all be long gone by now, given the negative things we are guilty of imagining at times.

Imagination can create reality, but only when we imagine deeply enough and consistently enough and feel strongly enough throughout our body that what we imagine is true. That is why fear is such a potent stimulator of imagination. It packs a powerful feeling punch on all three levels: spirit, mind, and body.

If we could imagine the things we would love to experience with the same energy that we imagine the things we fear, we would enjoy the most blissful experiences.

What I have discovered, both in my own life and while watching my clients' lives for many years, is that our imaginations work best on the things we focus on all the time, the things we dwell on, repeat, and reiterate with our own spoken or written words. They even work when we are not particularly paying attention to what we are saying or doing.

I just realized this today when I noticed that, for the past five years, one of the security questions on a website I visit often has been, "Where would you most like to live?"

My answer was "Paris," a dream of mine for years.

I was logging on to my account and the security question popped up. As I typed in the word "Paris," I realized that it was exactly where I now lived.

I laughed when I realized this.

Typing in that answer over and over for the past few years had brought it about.

(I have changed the security question and answer since then, by the way. The new one is: "Who is your best friend?" The answer is: "The Dalai Lama.")

IMAGINE THIS . . .
JUST FOR FUN BOOSTER

Create 10 of your own imagined security questions and answers.

Here are a few suggestions to get you started:

- What is your favorite place to vacation?
- Where do you want to live?
- What is your dream job?
- Who loves you?

You get the idea. Let this be fun.

Put these questions and answers in a prominent place, where you see them daily, like on the bathroom mirror or on the back of your cell phone case. Read them every day until it becomes automatic. Don't think about it after that. Just allow the magic to happen.

FEAR OF FAILURE

Often I run into people who tell me that they simply don't know what their heart's desire is. Their imaginations are so shut down that they can't clearly focus on what to create, leaving them feeling frustrated and at a loss, even though they believe that if they did know what they wanted they could create it.

I believe the problem here is that, once again, fear has gotten in the way. They are so used to avoiding fear that they have shut down their imaginations altogether. I also have come to observe in working with clients for so many years that one of the greatest fears people hold is the fear of failure. It is so huge that they don't allow themselves to dream of anything because they fear it just might not work out and they don't want to risk failure. This is crazy thinking, and often learned.

For example, I had a friend, Tom, whose father was so risk-averse that he warned all his kids, Tom included, never to take on risks or dream big, but rather to stay close to home, not expect a thing, and play it safe.

As a consequence of such imagination-squelching control, all seven kids, Tom among them, lived very cautious, uninspired lives, and found themselves filled to no end with frustration and boredom. When I tried to ask Tom what he wanted in life after yet another long session of complaining, all he could say was, "I have no idea. Just not what I have now."

I found a way to get around this imagination road-block and suggested it to Tom. It's the exercise that follows. I call it "Diving for Gold." This tool is an imaginary exercise that has you dive deep into your heart and helps you sneak past your fears to get in touch with what is truly important, just hidden. It helps you get in touch with your authentic yearnings and brings them back to life. If you aren't clear about what you want to create in life, try this exercise and see what you discover.

Diving for Gold Jump Start

Begin by looking around the room and breathing in deeply a few times. Once you feel relaxed, get your phone out and set the alarm to go off in three minutes.

Then close your eyes and, with the next breath, allow your attention to shift from your head to the center of your heart. Once you find yourself in your heart space, imagine connecting with your spirit, your true self. Imagine that your spirit is now going to lead you to your true desires.

Breathing in, with eyes closed, respond to the following, out loud, over and over again, until the timer goes off.

"If I weren't afraid, I would . . . [fill in the blank]."

When the timer goes off, take a final in-breath and relax. Notice how it feels to allow your heart to speak freely, unblocked by fear. Relax and notice how peaceful you feel.

Then pay attention to the things you mentioned and how expressing them has left you feeling. Often they stir the heart deeply. Sometimes this tool even brings up lots of tears. I believe it is because it reveals your true hidden heart's desires, and speaking this truth out loud brings about a deep sense of relief. It gives voice to the real you.

What is more exciting, however, is my discovery that consistently speaking openly from the heart like this has an attracting power of its own. It is so powerful that it can actually attract your heart's desire like a magnet.

IT'S NEVER TOO LATE

One client, Ellen, a 68-year-old recently retired nurse, used this tool to attract a new boyfriend into her life, and was really shocked when it happened. For years she bought into the idea that she was too old to find love, and besides, felt that all the "good men" were taken and the ones left over weren't worth spending time with. And yet, when she said for the first time out loud, "If I weren't afraid I would . . . ," to her great surprise what came out of her mouth was "meet a wonderful man and fall in love."

She couldn't believe she said that because she had long told herself—and anyone else who would listen—that she was quite content being single after going through a terrible divorce 23 years earlier.

Ellen didn't expect to say "fall in love," but once she did, she realized that it was true. This is exactly what she secretly longed for but was too fearful to admit.

Intrigued, she decided to loosen the reins of her fear a little and repeated this exercise every day while in the shower, as I had suggested. Each day she did it, she seemed to shift a little in her own behavior, and that too surprised her.

For one, she started accepting invitations to do things with friends, which she normally turned down. She was asked to join a bridge club and found that she thoroughly enjoyed being a part of it. Ellen was also asked to go with a friend to a new church, which she agreed to do, although she had repeatedly turned her friend's invitation down before this. This too she surprisingly loved.

There she met a woman who asked if she would like to join their church's foreign film club, something else Ellen was interested in but had never bothered to pursue. She agreed to that as well. It was there that she met Harold, a widower who had lost his wife to cancer a few years earlier. He was funny, warm, clever, kind, and most of all, very interested in her.

Ellen couldn't believe it. After only one month of Diving for Gold she had a male companion for the first time in more than 23 years.

All she said to me while blushing was, "I really found gold in Harold. I never imagined that a treasure existed before I started Diving for Gold. Wow!"

BACK TO YOU
DIVE FOR GOLD BOOSTER

Every day for three minutes for the next few weeks, Dive for Gold and see how it affects you.

To make it easier you can Dive for Gold while taking your morning shower as I suggested to Ellen, or while in the car if you drive to work. Or at any other time when you have three minutes to yourself and can speak freely. Each time you use this tool you may find yourself finding new "gold," a different set of heart's desires than the day before. But I have discovered that more often than not, the same ones keep turning up. These are usually your most heartfelt and authentic dreams that you have been hiding from the longest.

When Diving for Gold, don't worry about how these yearnings will come about. Just let your heart speak, out loud, for the full three minutes a day, and see what happens.

What I have observed over the years is that this tool guides your imagination around the roadblock of fear and leads it straight back to your deepest and most authentic heartfelt desires. And the more regularly you use it, the more both your imagination and your energy free up and naturally begin to move in the direction of your dreams, while at the same time attracting energy from the Universe to help you achieve them.

Don't Ask How

For years I wanted to meet David Bowie, as he was one of my all-time favorite rock stars.

I remember telling all my friends that one day I would meet him shortly after his iconic album *Aladdin Sane* was released when I was a teenager. I was obsessed with this dream.

I was so into David Bowie that my best friend at the time, Randy Roberts, and I even painted our faces the way Bowie had painted his on the album cover. We went out dancing looking like that almost every weekend for months.

I took this dream to an all-new level of desire when he released the song "Heroes" on a later album. This was my theme song. I didn't just hear this song. I felt it and lived it in my heart.

After that, I assured anyone who would listen to me that I was going to meet him and tell him in person that he was my hero. People laughed.

A little later, I became a flight attendant. One day I was working a flight from Chicago to Philadelphia and guess who was on my flight—and seated in my section?

It was David Bowie, flying incognito in coach class, row 23, aisle seat.

I nearly passed out when I saw him. I didn't want to make a scene, and couldn't because I could lose my job, but I nearly peed in my pants from excitement as I put down his meal tray. Too scared to say anything at first, I only walked by him and grinned like an idiot 20 times. But when I picked up his tray just before landing, I had to speak up. It was my last chance.

I leaned over and said, "I am such a huge fan of yours it is embarrassing. Meeting you has been one of my biggest dreams. My name is Sonia. Would you mind giving me an autograph if I am discreet?"

He smiled and winked and said, "Bring me a piece of paper."

He not only gave me his autograph, he drew a little design on it as well, and wrote on it that I was invited to the concert he was giving that night in Philadelphia. He whispered, "Just show this at will call. I'll let my manager know you are coming."

It doesn't end there. A few years later I made friends with another well-known musician in Chicago who invited me to see David Bowie in concert as his guest for my birthday. After the show he took me backstage and again I met David Bowie. This time we were actually introduced and talked for several minutes. I then met his band members and ended up having a few as clients thereafter.

I was devastated when David Bowie died of liver cancer so unexpectedly in January 2016. Since he reached even greater heights as a musical icon around the world following our first meeting, I feel more privileged than ever to have actually had the chance to meet and speak with him in person while he was alive. His creative spirit serves as a great and continual inspiration to me to this day.

THE IMAGINATION TO FORGIVE

When I first moved to Paris after my divorce, I was a mess. I was so hurt and angry with my ex-husband that I spent a great deal of time crying and feeling very wronged, not to mention wounded to my very core.

I thought, and said, and even screamed out loud at times, "How could you?" when thinking about what had just happened. I was shattered, shaken, deeply broken, and angry with myself, my ex-husband, and God, all at once.

I thought I had gotten over my resentments when I completed my pilgrimage, but that was before my ex-husband suddenly decided to ask for a divorce instead of trying to heal our marriage as he had said he wanted to do.

If I had been honest with myself, I would have acknowledged that I knew deeply and intuitively that on a soul level our divorce was in both of our best interests and in alignment with our souls' highest good. But that did not make it any easier for me to accept. Not one bit.

The truth was I didn't want to get a divorce. I felt tricked and wronged and even dumped by Patrick's decision to bring this about, and I was so resentful I could often barely get through the day.

I knew this resentment wasn't good for me, my daughters, or him, for that matter, but still it was how I felt.

One day I said to a friend on the phone quite spontaneously, "I cannot imagine ever getting over this," and the minute I heard my own words, I knew that was exactly what I had to do, and it was time to do it.

The only problem was that I had to forgive my ex-husband first. And I didn't want to. It felt too deliciously painful to be angry and wronged and wounded. In retrospect, I realized all of these feelings were just a way to hold on to what was no longer in my life, but at the time, I wasn't clear about that.

I just felt that I was a spiritual failure, and a loser at that, and that he had caused this.

Fortunately, being in Paris kept me from being completely swallowed into a huge sinkhole of pain, because it was just too interesting and beautiful to get lost in my wounds for too many hours a day. Thank God.

My despair and anger mostly erupted at night, when everything was quiet. It seemed to come in waves, leaving me floundering for higher ground and not succeeding. Fortunately, the waves began to subside over time, and nearly a year after the divorce, I knew in my heart it was time to let go, to forgive the past and move on.

I felt it with every cell in my body and every breath I took. But still I couldn't quite imagine how I was going to do that, even if it was clearly what I must do.

I needed some help to forgive. I wasn't managing well on my own. That was when it occurred to me to ask my spirit guide, Mary Magdalene, for help to forgive. I thought if Mary Magdalene could forgive all the horrors that she faced during her lifetime, then perhaps she could help me forgive my own personal horrors as well.

I began talking to her nightly in my imagination. I told her how hurt I was and how hard it was to forgive, even though I knew I must. I wanted to truly forgive and not just force myself, or guilt-trip myself into forgiving because I knew it was what I ought to do.

I poured out my heart and soul to her in my nightly imaginings and told her how, underneath the hurt and anger, I was really just scared and lonely.

I asked her, night after night, to soothe my heart and teach me what I needed to learn so that I could forgive and move on in peace. I asked her to heal my wounds and release my judgments. Not just those I held toward my ex-husband, but the more intense ones I held against myself.

I asked her to ask God and Mother Mary to come to my aid and relieve my pain. And then I would imagine her wrapping me up in unconditional love and lifting all the pain from the depths of my soul as I slept.

While all of this happened in my imagination, my experience with her was real. I felt her energy touching my wounded soul and slowly healing my heart. I felt her kindness and love for me, and for my ex-husband as well.

Above all, I felt her compassion surround my heart, slowly relieving me of my grief. By Christmas, my feelings began to shift. I had started to find the peace I had been praying for. What I had been imagining nightly for over a year now was beginning to take place.

I went for a walk one day, just three days after Christmas, and suddenly I realized that my imagined conversations with Mary Magdalene had been successful. All the pain and anger toward my ex-husband had vanished and was replaced with a deep forgiveness for both of us and for all the mistakes we had both made.

I was no longer angry or even wounded. I was free. I only wished my ex-husband the best, and myself as well. I imagined that all was in divine order and that in the end we were still connected on a soul level. We just had to move on with our respective paths, which were no longer the same.

Thank goodness for my imagination and the ability it gave me to talk to Mary Magdalene all those painful nights. Without her as my confidante and healer, I am sure I would still be in pain and struggling to forgive to this day. With her help, I was able to imagine forgiveness and allow it to occur.

It wasn't a quick creation. It took time and patience. But when I was finally able to forgive, it was complete, and I was overwhelmed with joy. I felt whole again—something that at one time I'd never imagined possible.

ASK FOR HELP JUMP START

If you really want to transform your life, I encourage you to use your imagination and ask for the help you need from those in angelic spirit realms, just as I did. By asking for help forgiving the people and situations that have harmed or hurt you in the past, you can find the relief and peace of heart and soul that you deserve.

The first thing to do is stop going over and over again in your mind the injuries that you have suffered. It is hard enough to take the first blow to your heart. Don't deliver the second blow yourself. I know. I've shot myself enough times with a poison arrow to know this never, ever helps you heal.

We do this by blaming ourselves, condemning ourselves, and shaming ourselves for being in pain. We overthink and feel as though we somehow deserve to be in such pain.

Instead of using your imagination this way, imagine instead that God loves you just as you are. Imagine that you are a beautiful spirit going through a difficult soul experience, but that your angels and guides and the Holy Mother-Father God love you unconditionally and are with you as you go through it.

Pray for help in imagining this is true. Use the super power of imagination to talk to your divine helpers and tell them what is in your heart. Ask for their help in healing. Ask for comfort. Ask for relief. The divine ones hear you, and will answer.

In addition, seek support from "believing eyes," friends who can assure you that you are lovable no matter what.

Seek counseling if you are really stuck, as you may need a professional to help free your imagination from negative self-talk, shaming, and blaming.

We humans are all wounded in some way, and because of these wounds, we wound others with our behavior at times. This is not an excuse for hurtful actions, but it is the truth. We often don't realize how hurtful we can be, and just as often are dumbfounded at how hurtful others can be. That is why it is so powerful to use our imaginations to practice forgiving and to ask for help in forgiving.

Take your time. Believe forgiveness is possible and will come in its own time. Pray for help to find self-love and for patience until you do.

And then expect good things.

CONCLUSION

I hope that by now the wheels of your imagination are rolling along and you are now actively starting to imagine a beautiful life of your own. Recognizing that you have already demonstrated having and using this super power in the past, you are now ready to direct this tremendous super power toward manifesting new and marvelous creations yet to come. As with meditation, imagination is free, unlimited, and priceless.

Imagination is a magical resource that will make every aspect of your life feel far more exciting, fulfilling, and satisfying.

Most of all, have fun with your imagination, and give it the time and space it needs to develop. Don't ask others for their opinions. Instead, turn inward and imagine your own possibilities.

General Tips for Successful Imagining:

- *Create the time to imagine—turn off the TV and computer.*

- *Imagine using all of your senses—sight, sound, smell, taste, touch, and feeling.*

- *Don't allow others to squelch your dreams.*

- *Acknowledge your successes and good creations daily.*

- *Have fun.*

With the restoration of your active imagination, you will soon discover that it can be exciting and fun to create. No matter how you feel about your potential right now, be open and receptive to noticing and believing in new and much more empowering ways of seeing yourself and your life. Soon you will be having the best time attracting what you really want instead of feeling left behind or left out. I promise.

Now that you have discovered the joy of imagining, you are ready to move on to activating Super Power #3: Intuition. Combining meditation with imagination, you are now more prepared than ever to reawaken this natural power and put it immediately to work for you. As you have learned, meditation quiets the mind enough to interrupt our habitual (and often negative) thought patterns and creates the space to begin to imagine once again in wonderful, creative ways, just as you did when you were a child. The way you are designed to imagine.

Imagination turns your world into one of open doors and possibility. It ignites your creativity as it delights your inner child. It helps you see beauty both inside and out. It makes life wonderful once again.

These combined energies, meditation and imagination, prime you for learning how to successfully tap in to your intuition and enter the gorgeous flow of your life. So now that you are ready, let's get to it.

Your Third Best Super Power:
INTUITION

Intuition is our natural GPS, our internal guide, our radar, our protection, our truth serum, our connector, our inner light, and the voice of our Higher Self. It is our internal hotline to our angels and spirit guides, and the divine Mother-Father God who loves us unconditionally and forever. Intuition is the divine intelligence we all possess that helps us to find our place and fulfill our purpose in this magnificent and holy Universe that we live in.

Intuition is our greatest super power of all, yet it only becomes consistently available to us through the exercise of our two other super powers, meditation and imagination. It completes the trilogy of divine powers we are gifted with in order to become masters of our human journey.

Intuition shows us how to make possible all that we imagine and all that we connect with in our meditation practice. Once our two other super powers clear our minds, open our hearts, set our intentions, and move us to create something new, our intuition leads us to the right people, the right places, and the right moments to bring our dreams to fruition.

Our intuition guides us to our divine purpose, leads us away from things and people that do not serve our highest good, and shows us the way to get from where we are to where we truly want to be.

MY STORY

In my family, when I was growing up, intuition was considered the first and most important of all our senses. My siblings and I were taught by my mother that we have an inner light in our hearts that guides us through life and that we must always follow, no matter what. We were trained from the earliest age to pay attention to the subtle signals that intuition gives us—a tightening in the chest, a buzzing in the heart, an inclination to back away instead of move forward, a hesitation when hearing something that doesn't quite ring true—and never argue with or doubt what we felt. The way was simple: "Always trust your vibes."

We could manage to get by in life without the help of our other senses, she insisted, but not without our intuition. She was living proof, as she had lost her hearing as a result of a sickness she contracted as a child.

Unable to physically hear, she was nevertheless clearly attuned to everything that went on around her, thanks to her intuition. It protected her after she became separated from her family during an evacuation from her home in Romania, when she was only 12 years old, during WWII.

She credited her intuition with helping her stay alive in spite of countless life-threatening situations, including the horrors of life in a German prisoner-of-war camp. It continued to be her guiding light long after she was liberated by the Americans. Alone in a foreign country, with few skills and little means of surviving, she was guided by her intuition to find food, shelter, and most of all, friendships that sustained her.

Trusting her intuition eventually led her to meet my father when she was 15. At 16, she married him and came with him to America. There they had seven children.

When growing up, her intuition was the cornerstone of our family's safety and security. Whenever her intuition said yes, it was all systems go. Whenever it said no, it was useless arguing. All too often we saw how accurate her "vibes" were, so we knew to listen without question. Whether or not we liked it, her intuition was spot-on, and her resolve that we all follow it was unshakable.

Because intuition was such a super power in her own life, she insisted it become the same for us. Instead of turning to others—including her—for guidance, she told us to ask our hearts and spirits for direction.

As a teenager, I was once asked by my best friend Vickie to go to a party that was being thrown by a kid from another school across town whom I didn't know at all. When I asked my mom if I could go, she hesitated and then looked me in the eye and said, "Before I answer, why don't you check in with your own vibes, Sonia? Do you think it is a good idea?"

Honestly, I didn't. The kid throwing the party had a bad reputation and was known to be involved with drugs. I told my mom I needed a minute to do that and went back to my room, where Vickie was waiting for me, eager to hear if I was allowed to go or not. I told her what my mom had said.

"Great, that means we can go," she said excitedly.

"Not really," I answered. "I really don't have good vibes about it, Vickie. Maybe I shouldn't go."

Familiar with my vibes, she groaned. "You and your vibes are so lame. It's supposed to be the best party of the year, and I worked so hard to get us invited. You have to go. Nothing will happen. Come on, just go."

I wanted to, but still, I didn't feel right about it. I had bad vibes.

"No, I don't think I should go," I finally decided. "It doesn't feel right."

Vickie was thoroughly annoyed with me when I said that and tried to change my mind, but without success. I knew what bad vibes felt like in my heart, and I was too scared to ignore them.

Vickie kept trying. "You'll miss a great party. I can't believe you aren't going."

I couldn't believe it either. I wanted to be cool and not miss a great party. But I also didn't want something bad to happen to me, especially if I'd been warned. I couldn't take the risk.

That night, Vickie went to the party without me. Apparently, the kid's parents were out of town and the party escalated out of hand. There was pot everywhere, which in the seventies was seriously against the law. The neighbors called the cops, who showed up and busted the party around 11 P.M.

My friend Vickie, along with a dozen or so other kids, was arrested for possession of pot and taken to jail, where her mom had to bail her out. Vickie got into a tremendous amount of trouble and had to have a lawyer get her off the hook. In the end she was sentenced to a year's probation and community service, and had an arrest on her record.

Sitting at a coffee shop shortly after this ordeal occurred, she shook her head at me and said, "Good thing you didn't go, Sonia. I only wish you hadn't let me go either."

That day sealed the deal for me. After what happened to Vickie, I decided would always listen to my vibes, no matter how pressured or tempted I would be not to. Ever since then, my intuition has been my hotline to personal power, safety, and guidance on every matter.

I do not know what life would be like without this super power to help me. In fact, I don't know how anyone can truly feel safe, secure, grounded, and guided without their intuition on board. We are naturally endowed with this super power and designed to use it. It is part of our basic human operating system. We need it to succeed in life.

Fortunately, unlike the other five senses, we cannot lose this super power. We can ignore it, deny it, undervalue it, mistrust it, even fight against it. But we cannot lose it. It exists in the center of our heart. As long as our hearts are beating, we are intuitively guided to be our true and best selves. It is simply up to us to pay attention to this super power and follow what we feel in our hearts.

I thank God I was taught to do this from the beginning. It is not only the foundation of my own life, it is my life's purpose to teach this essential truth to as many people as possible, just as I was taught.

Being disconnected from our intuition is like trying to find our way through a dense, fierce jungle at night, without a flashlight, and with no protection. It leaves us lost in the dark and at the mercy of our limited, often frightened, overreactive, and misinformed egos. We become stressed and suspicious of everything and everyone around us. Without our inner guiding light, all too often we become defensive, drained, and depleted. We lose our way and futilely struggle to find our security and sense of worth in the approval of others. We distrust and abandon ourselves, feeling we can only find safety by pleasing those whom we perceive to have power over us, leaving us feeling disingenuous, exploited, betrayed, wounded, and angry.

Our intuition frees us from this wasteful anxiety and uncertainty. It reminds us of who we are, and reveals to us how to express our authentic natures, successfully create the lives we yearn for, and be safe and protected in every part of our lives.

Without this super power at the helm of our lives, guiding us as it is designed to do, we end up living far beneath our fullest potential, often missing open doors of opportunity, ignoring our true callings, focusing only on surviving as opposed to thriving as empowered, creative, and joyful divine beings.

INTUITION IS NATURAL TO ALL OF US

We are all born with intuition. It is the intelligence of our knowing heart, the organ that keeps us alive. More than just a physical organ, the heart is also our first brain, the place where our spirit descends into our body and brings us to life. With every beat our heart speaks to us. Not only does it energetically inform and guide us in how to remain faithful to our true nature, but it also reveals the true nature of the world around us.

Through subtle vibrations that originate in the heart and move outward through the body, our intuition tells us whether or not we are on the right track. It gets our attention in many ways. We may feel it as an inner voice, a subtle tightness in the chest, a rumbling in the gut, a restriction in our throats, goose bumps on our arms, tension in our temples, restlessness in our legs, or some other physical sign. It knocks on the door of our attention through our nervous system and borrows our other senses when it speaks to us.

Because we are unique individuals, intuition shows up in our lives in unique ways. Some people perceive their intuition through visions. Others get intuitive hunches or feelings. For some, intuition shows up through sudden inspired ideas. Some connect with their intuition in dreams. Some hear an inner voice. Others just intuitively sense or know what is right or true for them though a general, overall, inexplicable knowing.

TUNE IN TO THIS . . .
INTUITION IS SUBTLE JUMP START

Stop for a moment and recall any intuitive experiences you may have had in the past. Don't look for something dramatic. Intuition is far more often experienced in subtle ways that, if noticed, can make a big difference in how you interact with the world. For example, can you recall a time when you suddenly thought of someone, only to have that person call you or run into you soon after?

Have you ever had a certain feeling that told you to change how you usually go to work, only to find your customary route blocked by an accident?

Have you ever had a bad feeling about someone and then discovered that he or she was dishonest or harmful to you?

Have you ever suddenly felt you needed to connect with someone, only to have that person become one of the most important people in your life?

Get out your small journal and list a few of your more memorable intuitive experiences. Recall as any details as possible.

(Hint: If you cannot recall any intuitive experiences off the top of your head, sit with friends or family and recall intuitive moments together. Hearing about others' intuitive experiences often jogs our own memories.)

INTUITION IS A PHYSICAL BOOSTER

In order to strengthen this natural super power, begin by noticing how intuition gets your attention in your body. Either answer out loud, or write in your journal the answers to the following:

Does your intuition come across as a flash in your mind?

Does it rumble around in your gut?

Do you get an overall sense pulling you toward or away from someone or something?

Do you experience tightness in your throat?

Does the hair on the back of your neck or on your arms stand up?

Do you feel a general positive or negative feeling throughout your body, especially the area of your heart?

Do you "hear" an inner voice?

Does intuition show up in your body in another way?

Once you consciously notice how your intuition manifests in your body, you naturally start to pay more attention to these signals when they arise.

INTUITION FOLLOWS YOUR
NATURAL INTERESTS AND PRIORITIES

Intuition signals us most often and most strongly in the areas that matter most to us. For example, mothers often have a keen intuition when it comes to the safety of their children.

People who work in finance often have a sixth sense about investing.

Fiction writers often receive what they call intuitive "downloads," in which entire stories, along with characters, drop into their awareness from out of nowhere. The same goes for other types of artists as well. Musicians intuitively hear the music they eventually score. Painters see visions that end up on canvas.

Some doctors intuitively sense what is wrong with their patients before the tests come back. Scientists who follow their instincts and hunches end up making huge breakthroughs in scientific understanding.

Builders can often immediately sense whether the ground under their feet is solid enough to build on with just a glance.

The professional athlete turns his body toward the ball before his eyes see where it is going.

Detectives follow their hunches when tracking crimes.

We all seem to have a sixth sense in the areas we love most.

Tune in to This . . .
What Areas of Interest
Do You Love the Most?
Jump Start

In your small journal, list your top interests and priorities. Think of the things you attend to first in life, and the things you put your time into, especially when it is your free time.

Now list times when intuition played a role in these areas For example, if you put your time into advancing your career, list any moments when your intuition assisted you. If you put your time into your relationships, list moments when you felt your intuition guided you in these relationships. Do the same in all the areas of your life that are important.

DON'T FIGURE IT OUT ... FEEL IT OUT

Intuition is not a faculty of your brain. It is a function of your heart, the feeling and sensing part of your nature. That is why trying to logically "figure things out" when looking for direction and answers that are not factual or yet clear often leads to a dead end.

Left-brain reasoning works well in many areas, such as when making computations, retrieving facts, drawing logical conclusions, or reading a map, so of course we must use this faculty of the brain when appropriate.

It is just that it's not always appropriate. Sometimes, facts may not yet be known. Furthermore, the "facts" we work with at times are not always accurate. They might be opinions and biases presented as or assumed to be facts. Prejudices are, more often than not, other people's beliefs and fears disguised as facts, handed down and accepted as true.

This is where intuition steps in to serve us. It draws information primarily through the intelligence of our hearts and shares with us what the left brain cannot tune in to. Intuition informs when the facts are not present, not accurate, not fixed, and especially not true. It reveals the hidden nature of the world around us, within us, and beyond us.

Intuition bridges the physical and nonphysical worlds, the known and the unknown. It connects us to nonlocal awareness, things that are out of sight, out of mind, and even out of this physical world. In other words, intuition connects us to the world of energy, the world of spirit, especially our own spirit, including our angels, our spirit guides, and our Creator, the Holy Mother-Father God.

Intuition reveals the unseen, the not yet obvious, not yet decided, and not yet—or ever—physically evident side of life. It makes clear what is unclear to the logical brain. It reveals what is not yet apparent to the eye. It exposes what is hidden or swept out of sight. It gives us clues to draw from, to learn from, and to guide us as we navigate our way through life. That is why it is so important to have intuition. It keeps us protected and connected to all that is true and meaningful to our purpose, our loves, our safety, our security, and our success.

It may be *different*, but it is not *difficult* to consciously tune in to your intuition once you learn how. The most direct way is to simply ask your heart, out loud, what it feels in any given situation. Then answer out loud. When answering, *feel* the vibration of your heart. Pay attention to how expansive, open, authentic, and true the response from your heart feels. Intuition, when expressed out loud, resonates in every cell as true.

INTUITIVE DECISION-MAKING BOOSTER

Close your eyes for a moment and focus on a specific issue or concern that leaves you feeling uncertain, unclear, or confused.

Now formulate this uncertainty into a question.

For example, you may wonder if you should move from one job, or even career track, to another. Perhaps you are unhappy in your present job, but you hesitate to quit or change direction because you are afraid to risk losing your job security.

To complicate matters, you have been offered another job in a different field, which interests you, but the security is less assured and you are less experienced in this area.

You may also have financial responsibilities, such as a mortgage to pay or children to support, so you worry if the new job will pay enough to meet your bills. The change appeals to you, but you just cannot get a clear sense of what to do.

Start by posing your question as succinctly as possible without using the word *should*.

For example:

"What is the most authentic and supportive next step for my spirit (and my family or other responsibilities) at this time concerning my job (or whatever the situation you are questioning)?"

Next, allow your ego to answer the question with, "My head says . . ." Then fill in the blank, out loud. Repeat this process over and over again until there is nothing more to add.

As you speak, feel the energy coursing through your body. Notice how the voice of your ego leaves you feeling. Does it feel clear? Concise? Light? True? Or does it feel heavy? Dense? Contracted? Afraid?

When your head has nothing more to say, clear your energy. Take a deep breath and look around the room. Notice what you see right in front of your eyes, just as you did in the meditation section of this book. Then exhale.

Close your eyes and take another deep breath. As you exhale, allow your attention to drop from your head to the center of your heart. Then breathe in again, deeply, and let out the sound *Ahhh*.

Next, place your hand directly over your heart and answer the same question, only this time, begin with "My heart says . . ." and fill in the blank, out loud, over and over again. Breathe in deeply between answers, but don't take too long to answer. If you do, check to be certain that you are not back in your head. If you are, don't worry.

Simply take another breath and refocus your attention on your heart and try again.

Continue answering the same question from your heart until you feel quiet inside. Notice how it feels when your heart speaks. Is the energy the same or is it different from the head? Is the energy heavy or light? Is it open or closed? Does it restrict you or leave you feeling as though you have more inner space? Contracted or expanded?

Notice the difference in responses between your head and your heart. Which feels better? More truthful? More empowering? Listen to that.

RECLAIMING INTUITION

Most people have been influenced, both directly and indirectly, by the example of others throughout their lives, to ignore or deny their intuition and let their fears lead them in life. Some people have fallen so deeply into this habit that they are unaware that they even have an inner voice to guide them, let alone one they can reliably trust.

Reclaiming your intuition is a process. It is learned one step at a time. The following steps begin your journey along this empowering path.

BE OPEN TO YOUR INTUITION

The first step in activating your intuition is to *be open* to it. As obvious as this seems, most people are not. Being open to your intuition is like turning on the receiver in your heart so you are able to pick up the subtle energetic signals that intuition sends out. Unless you are open to your intuition, you miss these powerful signals altogether.

If the receiver in your heart remains in the "off" position, you sadly remain disconnected from the greatest of your natural super powers and are left to struggle in the dark.

I've asked many people how open they considered themselves to be to their intuition over the years. To my surprise, many say they had never even thought about it until I asked. This is often because no one in their family of origin ever talked about intuition, let alone encouraged it. Others have shared that in their childhood home, especially if it was a particularly conservative religious one, intuition was often viewed as negative and was openly discouraged, disparaged, and considered downright immoral, as crazy as this seems.

Still others say they learned to dismiss intuition as fluff and were taught to stick to the facts in life when making decisions.

I have a client named Dale whose family was highly intellectual. Dale's father, a college professor, openly dismissed his son's feelings—or anyone else's—and insisted that only logic should be used when making decisions in life. Because of this, Dale simply tuned out his intuition and followed the example he was given.

The biggest logical decision he made was to go into real estate after college, because at least to him, that was the fastest track to making big money while allowing him to be his own boss, and that was what he wanted more than anything.

Furthermore, his family had a long and successful history in real estate. Both his grandfathers and several uncles had owned successful real estate development companies in the past and lived quite prosperously because of it. It made perfect logical sense to Dale to follow in their tracks. After all, it was in his blood.

The only problem was that, while it was in his blood, it wasn't in his heart. He got his real estate license and found work at a local agency, but he had little passion for the job, and even less success.

Stubbornly, he held on tight to his logic and stayed the course, even though all the signs indicated that he was on the wrong track, both for earning money and being happy. Refusing to listen to his heart for guidance in how to redirect his life, he was stuck, unhappy, and broke. He wasted several years of his life shuffling along, barely making ends meet, and feeling less and less good about himself with each passing unsuccessful quarter.

His lack of success and enthusiasm for his life became tiresome for his girlfriend as well, and wore down her interest in him. He was not fun to be around, never had any money, and became critical of her as a way of downloading some of the self-criticism he no doubt secretly directed toward himself. Their relationship suffered, and reluctantly, she finally broke it off. His stubborn refusal to tune inward, listen to his heart, and consider a different path made for miserable company.

It was only when she broke up with him that he realized that maybe his logic was doing him no good. He loved her and had to admit that his plan for success wasn't working. While his brain had convinced him in theory that real estate was the best way to go, in reality it only led to one dead end after another.

He realized his mistake and convinced his girlfriend to give their relationship another chance. She agreed, only on one condition: that he see the limitations of his so-called logic and get back in touch with his feeling and intuitive side so he could make decisions that would work out better for him.

With the help of a talented therapist, he slowly began to rediscover the wisdom of his heart. It was brand-new territory for Dale, but he was intrigued. As this was so contrary to how he was taught, it was slow going. But it did seem to help and eventually pointed him in a totally new professional direction that he had never considered before. He remembered that he liked writing and had once had a passion for teaching. He started to consider going to graduate school to become a professor, and maybe even a part-time writer, which genuinely excited him, even though it seemed a less prosperous path. He still kept his real estate job for the time being, but it no longer remained the yellow brick road to the Emerald City of his dreams. He was still cautious, but had to admit that being open to his intuition was making a positive and welcome difference, and that was what he needed.

TUNE IN TO THIS ...
HOW OPEN ARE YOU TO YOUR INTUITION?
JUMP START

Get out your journal and answer the following questions:

Do you recognize intuition as your natural birthright?

Do you accept that your heart is an intelligent organ capable of soundly and reliably guiding you?

Do you feel comfortable talking about your intuition with others?

Did anyone in your family openly and positively talk about their intuition with you?

Did you or do you have any role models who emphasize the importance of using intuition in life? Who are they?

Did or do you have influential people who discourage you from using your intuition?

Was it when you were young? Today? If yes, who?

Given all the evidence now available that we all have a powerful sixth sense, are you willing to be open to your intuition?

Speak Up Booster

If being open to your intuition is new for you, it also helps to vocally affirm your decision.

Try using the following affirmations, out loud and often:

- I trust my vibes.
- I listen to my heart.
- I go with my gut.
- I trust my hunches.
- My heart guides me well.
- I respect my intuition.
- I trust what I feel.
- I follow my instincts.
- I check with my intuition before I decide.
- My heart says . . .

Affirmations like these not only acknowledge your super power, they also bring you into present time (notice that they are all in the present tense) and free you of the limiting beliefs imprinted upon you at an earlier, less empowered age.

Expect Your Intuition to Guide You

The second step is to *expect* your intuition to guide you. When you expect something, you look for it. You attract it. That is because expectation works like a magnet. You draw your expectations to you.

Gina and Rachel were sisters. Raised in an intellectually vibrant household, with brilliant parents who often invited guests from around the world to stay with them, the girls were exposed to exhilarating evenings of conversation and debate their entire life.

While this laid the ground for both girls to develop into brilliant thinkers themselves, they diverged in one area. Gina freely relied on her intuition in making her decisions, a talent she both observed in many of the guests at the table and developed on her own as a means of keeping up with the conversations she was allowed to listen to and participate in as a child and young adult.

She expected her intuition to guide her and as a result was never disappointed.

Her sister Rachel, on the other hand, relied strictly on her intellect for guidance and refused to allow intuition to play a role in her life. She admired the great professors and scholars who often visited their home and decided that she had no use for anything other than intellectual knowledge. She couldn't even understand what Gina was talking about when she referred to her intuition. Unless Rachel could intellectually validate something, it simply wasn't real to her.

Gina decided to be premed in college. Yet, just before taking her medical college admissions test, the MCAT, she realized that she was not on a path that suited her and quit. More interested in natural healing than medical doctoring, Gina followed her intuition and started down that path instead.

Her sister Rachel, a natural born singer, rejected her passion as an unviable career path and pursued studies in economics and public policy instead. As unhappy as this choice made her, she pushed on, eventually entering a PhD program at NYU.

Gina went on to develop a vibrant massage therapy and holistic healing practice, which she operated out of her home. She absolutely loved her work and flourished financially. She openly credited her success and professional contentment to her steady intuition, which she counted on to show her the way.

Rachel, on the other hand, struggled with job after job, hating most of those she took, and ended up quitting again and again because she was so unhappy. Due to the stress this caused, she developed one extreme medical problem after another over the years and was unable to finish her studies. Beside herself with stress and frustration, Rachel agonized over how to restore her health and find happiness at work.

Gina encouraged Rachel to quit trying to figure things out with her head and look to her heart instead to guide her. She reminded her of her love of the arts—of singing and performance—and suggested she look to that world for opportunities.

Rachel thought this was the most absurd piece of advice she could ever receive. "How can I count on something as elusive as that?" she argued. "How could I ever be certain those doors would open? They simply won't. I have to be real."

Gina continues to thrive. Rachel continues to struggle. They each got what they expected.

We usually receive what we expect to receive. When it comes to intuition, expecting to receive guidance amplifies your new open attitude and tunes your attention to intuition's subtle signals. Expectation motivates you to check in with your inner voice instead of ignoring it. Once you expect intuition to guide you, it miraculously does. It directs your attention to what you may have been ignoring. Expecting your intuition to guide you allows it to do what it is designed to do, which is help you.

I'm not alone in this conviction. Others have felt the same way.

"Intuition is always right in at least two important ways; It is always in response to something.

It always has your best interest at heart."

— Gavin de Becker, *The Gift of Fear: Survival Signals That Protect Us from Violence*

"Often you have to rely on intuition."

— Bill Gates

"Have the courage to follow your heart and intuition. They somehow already know what you truly want to become. Everything else is secondary."

— Steve Jobs, 2005 commencement speech at Stanford

"I research new ideas very thoroughly, asking a lot of people about their experiences and their thoughts. But on many occasions I have followed my intuition: you can't make decisions based on numbers and reports alone."

— Sir Richard Branson

"I've trusted the still, small voice of intuition my entire life. And the only time I've made mistakes is when I didn't listen."
— Oprah Winfrey

Follow their example in expecting your intuition to guide you to greatness as it has for them.

THERE IS ALWAYS A SOLUTION

Growing up I was taught, along with expecting good things, that no matter what challenge or problem I would encounter in life, there would always be a solution, and my intuition would lead me to it. With this assurance, I have fully expected to be led to a solution every time I needed one, even when it looked unlikely that it would show up, and on time. I've not been disappointed.

Once my three-month lease was running out on my less-than-luxurious apartment in Montmartre in Paris, I set out to find a more suitable place to live. I began by making a list of things I wanted to find in the new place and the price I was willing to pay for these things.

I went to several rental companies to begin my search and shared my list of requirements and the price I was willing to pay for them. I was told every time that it was not possible to find so many desirable features, such as a modern kitchen, a dishwasher, a washer and dryer, high ceilings, and sunlight, on a quiet street, for so little money. Some even looked at me as though I were crazy. What I was shown in lieu of what I wanted was worse than where I was. So I decided not to listen to the Realtors and to find my next apartment on my own. I asked my intuition to lead me to my new place and never doubted that it would,

YOUR 3 BEST SUPER POWERS

even if the time constraint was starting to feel a little intimidating.

One morning, just after enjoying a delicious cup of coffee at my favorite local café, I felt an urge to look on Airbnb again, even though I'd had such bad luck there before. It didn't make logical sense to do that either, because most Airbnb apartments are rented for short periods of time and I needed a long-term rental, as I had decided to make Paris my new home.

It didn't matter. My intuition said look again, so I did. This time I found a gorgeous apartment that really stood out among the rest, but was very expensive and offered only on a short-term lease basis.

Ignoring what the listing said, I requested a showing anyway. When I walked in I fell in love with the apartment right away. There were only two problems. It was quite a bit more money per month than I wanted to spend and there was only the short-term lease option available.

I told the Realtor I absolutely loved the place and asked her to ask the owner if he or she would lower the rent considerably and allow me to lease it for a year or two. "I really doubt that would be possible for such a lovely place as this, as it is rare to find," she shared, trying to discourage me, "but I will ask."

"Yes, please do," I urged. "And please tell the landlord that I would make a great tenant and bring the place positive energy as well." She laughed at that, clearly letting me know that this was the first time she ever heard something like that from a potential renter.

"I will let you know," she said when we parted, shaking hands.

I left feeling both excited and nervous. It was the nicest apartment I had seen since I'd begun looking, and I really felt I could comfortably live there and make it a home. While my mind was filled with tension, my intuition told me to relax and not to worry. It would all work out. I had to believe this as I now had only a week to find a place before my present lease expired, and no backup whatsoever.

Three days passed and finally I received a text from the Realtor. Apparently, after much consideration and reviewing my application, the owner of the apartment had agreed to my terms. He lowered the rent as I had asked and agreed to a long-term lease.

"It's unbelievable," the Realtor said. "I cannot believe he agreed to your terms. This never happens in Paris." Grateful, I signed the papers that day and moved in a few days later, just in time before my old lease ended.

My landlord and his wife turned out to be a genuinely warm, welcoming people and have since become two of my very good friends here in Paris. Once again, fully expecting my intuition to guide me to the right solution and being willing to withstand the pressure of others and the appearance of impossibility, I was rewarded with the perfect solution to my housing problem. I admit there were a few moments of doubt, especially when others asked, "What are you going to do if you don't find a place in time?" But deep down I expected the solution would reveal itself, as it had every time in the past.

It was a *miracle*, the word I use to describe the unlikely occurrences brought about by the grace of my intuition and the goodness of God, which happen just in the nick of time. Miracles bring bountiful and beautiful blessings. I've had many and expect many more.

Tune in to This . . . Intuitively Attracting Solutions Booster

Expecting your intuition to guide you may be a new habit you need to develop. Here are some tips to help you:

- Be clear on what you need guidance on and say so out loud.

- Make a list of what you want help finding.

- Have absolute confidence it will show up.

- Before making any decision, stop and say out loud, "Let me check in with my intuition. I'm sure it will guide me."

- Ask a question of your intuition as you sit in meditation. Then wait for the answer to come. It will.

- Listen with your whole body and expect it to tell you if something resonates as true or not.

- Slow down. Pay attention to your gut. Check in with your heart. Notice the energy you are presently feeling. Recognize it as your guide.

- Tell others you are intuitive, and make no apology for it.

- Ask your Higher Self for guidance. Then listen with your heart.

- Follow through on your hunches even if they make no sense.

- Don't confuse others' opinions with fact.

These little practices create the habit of expecting your intuition to guide you. The more you expect it, the more you notice your intuition because you are looking for it to show up.

Trust Your Intuition

The third step is to *trust* your intuition when it does show up.

Intuition is not all that elusive. Most people I've talked to sense or feel their intuition more often than they realize. The problem is, they do not believe in it enough to pay attention to it. Instead they ignore it, deny it, argue with it, or fight against it. In other words, they do anything but trust and follow their intuition, and consequently miss out when it could actually help them.

My client Louise, a successful 52-year-old real-estate broker in California, had an intuitive hit that the man she was dating was not quite the wonderful guy he presented himself to be. He was romantic, charming, loving, and attentive to her family, and as much of a gentleman as she ever hoped to find.

When her friends asked about him, she replied that he seemed "too good to be true," and a part of her actually felt this way. But because she loved his attention and was tired of being alone, she chose to ignore this nagging sensation. It surprised her that he proposed marriage to her, with a gorgeous diamond ring, only three months after they met.

She was flattered, but suggested to him that it was a little too soon to get married, as they hardly knew each other. He strongly disagreed with her, insisting that, at their ages, there was no reason to wait. He said he knew what he wanted and he wanted to marry her.

His campaign of persuasion overrode her intuitive hesitation and she reluctantly agreed. They married in Las Vegas two weeks later. Soon after the wedding her nightmare began.

He suddenly stopped behaving like a gentleman. He insisted she turn her financial affairs over to him, as he was now the "man of the house." He started to control what she wore, accusing her of being a "tramp" if she wore something he didn't approve of. He became rude, controlling, and jealous. In other words, he turned from Dr. Jekyll into Mr. Hyde.

In seven short months he made her life a living hell. Emotionally devastated but not totally surprised, as she'd had suspicious feelings about him from the beginning, she finally ran a background check on him, something she should have done the moment she had bad vibes.

She was shocked to learn that he was a serial con artist and had been married no fewer than eight times before, all to financially independent women whom he had fleeced.

Embarrassed that he had taken her for a ride as well, she immediately set out to divorce him. What followed was an ugly divorce and near-complete financial ruin.

"I am an intelligent woman," she lamented. "I knew in my heart something was wrong, but I got swept away with the romance and didn't trust my vibes. How stupid could I be?

"Never again," she swore to me. "Never again."

Many people have horror stories about not trusting their vibes. It happens for a lot of reasons. Like Louise, we have times when we are tempted to suspend listening to our intuition because we are seduced by the allure of something we want. We may be intuitively alerted that something is off, too good to be true, or not as it seems, yet we don't want to test the validity of our instincts, as we don't want to give up our illusion.

We sometimes suppress what we intuitively sense because we don't want the answers we seek. They are too painful to accept. So we ignore our sixth sense or deny it.

Katherine was married to a career military man who dedicated his life to protecting others. They had one son, David, who was a much gentler soul than her husband. But David wanted to live up to his father's expectation of being a "man," so followed in his footsteps and joined the Marines.

Clearly, this was not the best choice for him. He struggled every single step of the way and suffered emotionally because of it. Nothing about the Marines suited his soul. He failed tests, fought with his superiors, and fell into a deep depression. It was obvious to his mom and his wife of three years, but not to his father. He said David just needed to "man up" and quit his whining.

One day, David did not show up to his post. He had completely disappeared, but his car was found parked next to a bridge off of which people had been known to jump. Three days later they still couldn't find his body.

No one knew where David had disappeared to, and there was no concrete evidence that he had indeed jumped. His father had a nervous breakdown. Kathleen and David's wife nearly followed behind.

When Kathleen called me she was looking for answers. She said she was blank and couldn't see or feel her son anywhere. I listened, feeling heartbroken for her.

"Where is David?" she cried. "Where is he?"

I didn't say anything for several moments, letting the waves of her emotions move through her as they needed to, and when she was quiet I said, "Ask your heart, Kathleen. You know."

She was silent for a good minute before she said, "I do know. He is in heaven. It was too painful for him to live the wrong life, and he didn't know how to break free. He jumped that morning. I felt it the night before. I sensed his leaving as I brushed my teeth, but I put it out of my mind. I know that is true. I don't need his body to confirm that." Then she became quiet.

Once she acknowledged what she intuitively knew, she relaxed. As painful as it was to admit, ignoring the truth that her son had died was worse.

"I am now going to let myself grieve his loss," she finally said, filled with resolve. "It is better than pretending I don't know."

She thanked me and hung up. Her intuition would help her heal and find closure. There was still a long road ahead for her, but at least she could now begin that journey.

The tragedy in this family's story is one of ignoring intuition all the way around. David's father ignored his intuition so was not able to see or support his son's authentic spirit, and instead imposed a rigid set of standards for his son to live up to. Kathleen ignored her intuition and didn't reach out to David earlier to offer support in questioning his choices as she often felt she should have. David's wife ignored her intuition and pretended he was okay because he insisted he was, instead of insisting he face the truth and get help. And David ignored his own intuition and insisted on following a path that was clearly wrong and damaging to his soul.

The end result was loss and devastation all the way around.

Tune in to This . . .
Paying the Price Jump Start

One of the ways to prevent such soul tragedies is by acknowledging the price we pay for ignoring this essential super power of intuition. It becomes far more difficult to ignore our intuition once we honestly acknowledge the consequences.

Get out your notebook once again and answer the following:

When in the past have you ignored your vibes?

What price did you pay?

Is there anything you intuitively feel now but have no proof of?

Notice how you feel now that you have acknowledged these feelings as solidly as you have. Can you describe your feelings in words? Do you feel relieved? Satisfied? At ease?

Pay particular attention to your body and any changes in any area of your body.

Describe all these feelings, however subtle, as specifically as possible. Write them down in your notebook. The more you acknowledge your feelings, the more attuned to your intuition you become.

Fear of Trusting Your Vibes

We often don't trust our intuition because we are afraid it might be wrong. We have been conditioned to look only at the facts as we perceive them in the moment and to ignore or discount deeper feelings that signal that things may not be as they seem. We go along with what *appears* to be true instead of what we *feel* is true and ignore our inner alert system. We don't want to be the "spoilsport," or be considered crazy or ungrounded. So we push our intuitive feelings aside and go along with the general consensus. This always comes back to haunt us in the end.

Mark was intrigued when his friend and business partner, Donald, suggested that they merge their growing company with another.

According to the plan, if they merged with the other company, both he and Donald would stay on and continue to run the day-to-day operations. They would just not be in charge of the major company decisions. For this they would be generously compensated.

Donald was very enthusiastic and tried to persuade Mark that the deal was a win-win situation for them: more money, less stress. Mark listened, but something about the top brass at the other company didn't feel right to him. Nevertheless, Mark had to admit that he and Donald had both worked incredibly hard over the years and it would be nice to have some of that pressure taken off. Also, the money was very attractive—that, he couldn't deny. And he loved their business and the people who worked for them. In the end, Mark agreed to the deal despite his bad feeling about the people who ran the other company.

Less than a year into the merger, the new company CEO started selling the company off piece by piece. Despite what Mark and Donald had been promised, what they had built up over 20 years was now being taken apart in a matter of months. Employees who had given them years of devoted service as they were growing the company were now suddenly without jobs. While Mark and Donald had financially benefitted from the deal, it left both of them feeling morally bankrupt.

Mark blamed Donald for the debacle, which ruined their friendship. But in truth Mark knew it might have been different had he trusted his vibes and spoken up in the beginning. He secretly felt it was his fault that everyone lost their jobs, not Donald's. It caused him a lot of sleepless nights.

Tune in to This . . .
Name It, Then Claim It Booster

If you have not had much practice trusting your intuition, it is easy to understand how it might feel risky to do so.

Overcoming your fear is actually quite simple. Every time you get a "hunch," an "aha" feeling, a vibe, an instinct, a subtle warning, or a red or green light, simply write it down in your small notebook, or record it in some other way, such as on your smartphone.

In doing this, three important shifts begin to occur:

1. What you write down or record will start proving itself to be accurate, providing concrete evidence that your intuition is worth listening to.

2. When you make note of your intuitive feelings in a tangible way, either by writing them down or recording them, you place importance on these feelings. This action tells your subconscious mind that you are no longer ignoring your intuition. So your subconscious mind gets the message that intuition matters and sends even louder signals.

3. Once you write down your intuitive feelings, you will discover that you have many more intuitive insights than you were even aware of. Writing down your intuitive feelings opens the floodgates and lets more and more flow to your conscious mind. It's like opening the door to a treasure trove of insights.

These shifts, one following upon another, start to build a case for trusting your vibes. Moreover, it's a lot of fun.

Michael, a client of mine, decided to test this theory out. He began by asking his intuition what time the morning train, which he had to take to school and which was infuriatingly inconsistent, would arrive. If he miscalculated it by even a minute or two (which he often did), he would have to wait for the next one to arrive, and consequently be late for school.

The first time he asked himself when the train would arrive, he felt it would show up at 7:00 A.M. sharp. Making a note of it, he set his watch alarm to sound at 7:00, and set off to the station. The moment the alarm sounded at 7:00 A.M., the train pulled up. He was standing there ready to get on.

Surprised, yet needing more proof, when he got off to change trains, he again asked himself what time the connecting train (equally inconsistent) would show up. He intuitively felt it would arrive 13 minutes later. Again, he set his watch and waited. Just as the alarm sounded, the train pulled into the station.

Success twice in a row made him a believer. Even though these were small things, it was enough proof to make him pay more attention to his intuition when it came to bigger things.

TUNE IN TO THIS . . .
WRITE IT DOWN JUMP START

Once again get out your small notebook and answer the following questions:

What does your intuition tell you that up until now you have not fully acknowledged?

How long have you been feeling this?

Did any new insights show up once you started writing?

Even if what you recorded is uncomfortable to acknowledge, how does it leave you feeling? Just as in the last entry in your journal, describe your feelings as specifically as possible. The more specifically you can define how your intuition comes across, the stronger it becomes.

FIND A GOOD SOUNDING BOARD BOOSTER

In addition to recording your intuitive feelings, another highly effective way to start trusting your vibes is to find someone to serve as your sounding board and to share your intuitive feelings with that person.

Sounding out your intuitive feelings is powerful. The more you share what you intuitively feel, the more confident in trusting your intuition you become. Like the saying goes, "The more you name it, the more you claim it."

Choose someone who will support you, will listen without judgment, and will encourage you to trust what you feel.

Meredith knew it was time to leave her unhappy marriage. She and her husband were no longer communicating, and he was gone most of the time. She had been a stay-at-home mother and had not had a job in more than 20 years, ever since her children were born. In order to divorce, she had to find a means of supporting herself and was overwhelmed with anxiety about what to do.

Insecure about not having any viable skills outside of being a mother and homemaker, she feared that there was no way she could make the money she needed in order to live apart from her husband.

Meredith turned to a friend and shared her fears and confusion. Her friend listened and then asked her to name her talents instead of her fears. She began listing them, and before long she recognized that in addition to her mothering and homemaking skills, she also possessed the talent of listening, mediating, and solving family problems. From this she suddenly had an intuitive hit to look into family mediation. Everything about it felt right and resonated throughout her body as something she could excel in.

Though this career path had never occurred to her before, when sharing her insights with her friend, the idea popped into her head like a lightbulb. Following her "aha" insight, she discovered that there was a professional meditation training program happening in her city that she could enroll in right away. She signed up that day. Not only the idea, but also the timing was perfect, as it was only offered once a year and was beginning in two weeks.

Meredith believes that had she not turned to her friend as a sounding board, she might never have tuned in to this idea.

From my experience, exploring your inner world with a trusted friend often opens the door to your intuition. It takes this super power out of the proverbial "closet," hidden away in your heart and easy to miss, and brings it into the light of day, where you can openly explore possible answers and tap into your intuition as you do.

PULLING IT ALL TOGETHER: ACT ON YOUR INTUITION

Now that you have awakened your intuition by being open to it, expecting it to give you guidance, and trusting that it will steer you in the right direction, it is time to start acting on your intuition, because until you do, it doesn't do you any good. Most of us have had intuitive feelings that we have ignored or paid attention to only when it was too late, and suffered everything from small annoyances to huge, even life-threatening consequences because of it.

I have noticed that in most cases, acting on your intuition sooner rather than later makes all the difference in how much it helps you. In some circumstances, you have time to consider your intuition before you act on it. But most of the time, the sooner you listen to this super power the better off you will be in the long run. Most of the time I have found it is best to listen and act on intuition right away.

Rachel noticed a very small, almost imperceptible lump on her right breast and immediately had a troubled feeling about it. Her intuition told her to get it checked out as soon as possible, but she was so busy with her full-time job and raising her three children as a single mother that it was two months before she got to a doctor to have it examined.

Once the lump was biopsied, it turned out to be stage-two breast cancer. She was understandably upset, but not totally surprised. Kicking herself for having waited so long to get it checked out, she wondered if she might have had an even better chance of beating it if only she had acted sooner on her feeling. Now she will never know.

The decision to act on your intuition instead of pushing it aside can save you time, trouble, money—even your life. Time is often the most essential thing when it comes to having your intuition protect you. It often shows up to let you know something is off, or not right, and must be addressed immediately. Otherwise the problem continues, and the negative consequences keep growing.

Irina, a small workshop presenter, sat down at her computer in order to complete a project for work, but just as she was about to settle in, she got a strong feeling she should check her Facebook account, which she used to post ads for upcoming workshops. Annoyed that this thought had come up, she treated it as a distraction. She ignored her feeling and refocused on her work. Again, the nagging feeling returned, a little stronger than before. Choosing to ignore it for the second time, she tried to force her attention on to her project. Five minutes later, the nagging feeling to check her Facebook account returned once more, this time very insistently. Clearly, it wasn't something that would leave her alone, so she stopped what she was doing and opened up her Facebook account.

Once it was open, she was shocked to find that someone from Canada had hacked into her account and charged an ad in the amount of $200. Worse, the same person had ordered future ads for their services to be placed in the amount of up to $9,000 a day on the same account for the next week. She also discovered that whoever did this had also managed to make it impossible for her to stop the orders that had been placed and locked her out of the ability to make changes to the account. She immediately contacted Facebook to report the fraud.

Luckily for her, the larger charges were still pending and had not yet been processed, so she was able to close her account. Because she discovered this so quickly, there was little damage done.

Had it gone unnoticed, however, it might have proven far more difficult to intercept and would have caused far greater damage. It cost her a lot of time and effort to clear up the mess, but at least she caught it early enough that it did not cost her a lot of money as well. She was grateful that her intuition was so insistent and didn't allow her to ignore her feeling that afternoon, as much as she had wanted it to.

ENGAGE YOUR INTUITION IN LITTLE MATTERS FIRST

Acting on your intuition is easier if you exercise it often, starting with little matters, almost like a game, until it becomes comfortable and familiar. Daily intuition workouts strengthen these energetic muscles and help you fine-tune your intuition at the same time. Acting on your intuition in little nonthreatening ways makes it easier to act on your intuition in more significant matters when the time comes because you've established the habit of doing so already.

You can consult your intuition when you're in a crowded parking lot, for example, and searching for a place to park. Tune in to your intuition and ask it to guide you to the next open space. Then immediately follow your vibes to the open spot.

When waiting in front of a bank of elevators, stand in front of the door you feel will open up first. If you are correct, congratulate yourself. Remember the feeling that drew you to that elevator. If the elevator you chose, on the other hand, is not the correct one, just shrug it off, saying, "Oh well," and let it go. It's just a game, after all.

When you are wrong, check in and notice whether you truly *felt* correct about your intuition or if you were simply guessing. Often people admit that they didn't really tune in, but rather did just randomly guess the answer when playing this game. Guessing is not the same as acting on intuition. Guessing doesn't involve paying attention and tuning in to energy in motion. No wonder it is hit-or-miss.

It takes a little practice to get in the habit of acting on your intuition without hesitation. The more you practice in these situations where the outcome isn't of serious consequence, the easier it becomes.

TUNE IN TO THIS ...
SAY IT OUT LOUD BOOSTER

- When the phone rings, before you see caller ID, use your intuition to identify the caller. The instant you hear it ring, say out loud, "That's my boss," or "my husband," or "my daughter," or whoever you feel is calling before looking at the screen, if on a smartphone, or answering if you are on a landline. Then check to see if you are correct.

- When you receive a letter via snail mail, before opening it, tune in to the date it was written and say so out loud. Then open it. If you are not familiar with the return address, tune in to who wrote it. Was it a man or a woman? Were you able to tune in? A little? A lot?

- When you receive bills, before opening them up, tune in to the exact amount due. Do the same when filling up the car with gas, using your intuition to tune in to the exact amount of gas the car will take before you start pumping. Try it at the grocery store, when purchasing groceries. Tune in to the dollar amount you will spend before checking out. Did you accurately tune in? Did you *feel* your intuition or were you just randomly guessing? Are you able to tell the difference? Are you starting to get a feel for intuition coming through?

The point is to practice using your intuition in daily ways that are easy, fun, and offer feedback. This strengthens your intuition and at the same time engages you to act on it in nonthreatening ways.

Playing intuitive games such as these gives you the little nudge you need to start acting on your intuition automatically. If you do this often enough it becomes natural and begins to permeate all areas of your life.

The key is to not need to be "right," but to have fun as you develop this new skill.

Many students over the years have reported back how in playing little games like this they suddenly found themselves following their intuition more than ever before. Before they knew it, it had become the most natural thing in the world to do.

Ronnie, a mother of young two boys, ages 8 and 10, loved playing silly intuitive games with them, especially whenever they were in the car. They predicted the model of the next car that would travel in the opposite direction. Or they intuitively named the color of the car that would appear at the next red light. They intuitively searched for parking spots. They expanded their game to intuiting things on sale when they went to the mall. They tuned in to the name of the server at a restaurant. Their game expanded until it permeated everything they did together. They had fun with it and laughed as they learned. Eventually, they followed their intuitive clues without question on every matter. It became normal.

One night, they were in the car headed to their favorite Italian restaurant, Vince's, which they went to every Saturday night. On the way, Ronnie's older son, Michael, said, out of the blue, "My intuition tells me not to go to Vince's tonight. We have to go somewhere else."

Because they had been playing intuition games for months, Ronnie listened without question. She turned the car in a different direction and they went to get burgers instead.

They had an average meal and soon after, headed home. The next morning, Ronnie heard on the local news that there had been an outbreak of food poisoning among the patrons at Vince's the night before. More than 10 people ended up in the hospital, one a two-year-old child who was extremely sick and in intensive care. Ronnie and her boys were not among them, thank goodness.

TUNE IN TO THIS . . .
MAKE A NOTE OF IT JUMP START

Get out your notebook once more and in it write down the answers to the following questions as specifically as possible:

When in the past have you acted on your intuition? What did you feel? How intense or strong was it? Was it a big deal or a little deal that made a big difference in the flow of your day? What time of day was it? Who or what did it involve?

What was the outcome?

When has your intuition failed to be accurate? Were you emotionally involved at the time, and if so, with whom and in what way? Was it over something you wanted that didn't happen? Were you neutral or emotionally invested in the outcome?

Were you sensing your intuition or just guessing the outcome? Can you tell the difference? Can you describe it?

When in the past have you spontaneously acted on your intuition, yet never knew the reason for your feeling, and were glad you did? How did you feel after all was said and done?

As you write, notice the changes you feel in your body, your energy, and your mind.

Do you feel more in integrity with yourself? Do you feel more grounded? Do you feel more aligned with your spirit? Yes, or no, just pay attention to the shifts that occur when you freely acknowledge your intuition.

Tune in to This . . .
Intuitive Rocket Boosters

Here are some more simple yet powerful ways to get into the habit of tuning in your life.

- Name the next song coming up on the radio as you listen in your car.

- Announce the time before you look at your watch.

- Leave a place if it doesn't feel comfortable— you don't need a reason why.

- The moment you have a feeling to go in a different direction or to a different place, just do it.

- If you don't like someone, trust there is a reason.

- If you are suspicious of someone, trust there is a reason.

- If you feel someone is lying, trust your vibes.

- If you get an intuitive hit to call someone, stop what you are doing and call.

- If you get an intuitive feeling to change your plans, change them.

- If something doesn't seem right with your food at a restaurant, don't eat it. Send it back.

- If you get a positive feeling from someone, tell them.

- If you have an urge to cancel or change your plans, do so.

- If you get a bright idea to sign up for a class, sign up.

- If you have the hunch that you would be good at something, try it.

- If you feel you need to quit your job, start immediately looking for a new one.

- If you want to write a book or start another creative project, start today.

- If you feel you shouldn't have something in your diet, leave it out.

- If your body tells you to go to bed, go.

- If you need time alone, take it.

- If you get a feeling to check the tires on your car before a road trip, check them.

- If you have bad vibes about someone, walk away.

Acting on your intuition in all of these little ways builds up the inner muscles you'll need to act on your intuition in bigger ways in the future. Soon, acting on your intuition will be spontaneous and the only way in which you live because you will have such positive results.

Trust Your Vibes

Wherever you go, and whomever you are with, notice the energy and trust what you feel. Like a hound dog sniffing the trail, allow this innate super power to scan the energy of everything—*everything*—in your life to see what is real, reliable, and good for you. Make checking in with your intuition your daily habit, the default way you do things and make decisions, the means by which you accept or don't accept things; in other words, make it a normal part of your life.

Because I travel so much and need a good night's sleep, I always scan the energy of the hotel rooms I am given. If a room doesn't feel right, I call the front desk and ask for another. I don't feel the need to give a reason, but if I am asked, I simply say I have bad vibes in that room.

I have never had a single person argue with me when I give my reason. They either get it or think I'm crazy. In either case, they cooperate. Even when rooms are tight, I'm always given a new one. I don't need to know or explain why I feel the way I do. Just feeling it is enough for me. Let it be enough for you as well. It's liberating when you do.

When I enter restaurants, I do the same thing. If the vibe is off, I leave, even if I have already been seated. I don't feel the need to explain myself, and you shouldn't either.

I scan the food I eat. I scan the clothing I wear. I scan the places I go. I scan the people I am with. I scan the opportunities I am presented with. I scan the e-mails I read. I scan the conversations I have.

I am looking for the truth, for what is real, solid, reliable, and genuine *for me*. I look for what resonates with my spirit and is congruent with my heart and soul. I scan for support and look out for obstacles. I scan for openings and dead ends. Intuitive scanning is automatic for me, as if I have an inner GPS that is always switched on. I don't stop and think about it. I flow with my intuition. If I feel something, I trust it. I don't need to know exactly what it is that I am feeling or sensing. I simply pay attention to what my intuition tells me, and I don't ask questions.

Yes, it is risky at times, and no, there are no guarantees that your intuition will always be right. You may or may not receive confirmation that it is. But you will be more in charge of your life than ever. And that is what matters.

TUNE IN TO THIS . . .
CHECK IT OUT BOOSTER

Start using your intuition to scan the energy of everything in your life today.

- When shaking hands with someone, scan their energy so you get an accurate read on this person.

- When you enter a room, scan the energy to see if it is harmonious and grounded, or if instead it is filled with negative, dissonant energy, or bad vibes.

- When talking with someone on the phone, listen to more than their voice. Listen to their energy and vibration to get a clearer sense of what they are truly communicating or not communicating.

- When making purchases, big or small, scan the product to get a sense of whether it feels right, solid, and reliable for you.

- When making a decision, check in with your intuition before you commit.

- When listening to someone speak, listen for their meaning more than their words. Are they telling you the whole truth? Are they hiding or withholding something? Are they unsure? Are they reliable and trustworthy?

- When planning travel, scan the place you intend to visit to see if the energy feels propitious for you at this time. Will the weather be good? Will the hotel be okay?

- When feeling ill, scan your body for the real root of the problem.

- When taking medicine, scan to see if it is right for you.

- Scan everything every day.

You become more super empowered when you no longer feel the need for outside verification of whether or not your intuition is right. In your heart, you know. That is all you need. If it feels right to you, go with it. If it doesn't, walk away. In the end, it becomes that simple.

LIVING AN AUTHENTIC LIFE

While it is wonderful that your intuition can help find you find parking spaces, help you locate your keys, and even protect you from harm, the greatest reason why this is the most important super power of all is that it is the inner compass that guides you in how to live an authentic and meaningful life.

When we follow our intuition, we are moved by our spirit to make choices that support our deepest truths and our sense of purpose and bring us our greatest inner peace and joy.

It takes courage to use this super power. It is not for the faint of heart. In fact, the word *courage* comes from the French word *coeur*, which means "heart." To live with courage means to overcome your fears and follow your heart. While that may feel reckless to a logic-based person, it is the most intelligent thing a person can do. The heart is an intelligent, conscious organ, capable of guiding every step along our path. It steers us in the direction of our true desires and away from what is not true, not real, not safe, not the right way for us. Nothing feels better than when we live in accordance with our heart, as it brings about a sense of integrity and peace, and nothing is better for the world than that. The greatest gift we can offer the world is our happy, peaceful heart. It is contagious. But it requires courage.

I spoke to a client named Jason who lived in a rural community in Iowa and had made a great living developing equipment that helped efficiently provide water and other resources to the farmers in the area.

His company prospered for many years, but one day he woke up and knew in his heart that he no longer wanted to continue doing this work. It wasn't that it had been wrong for him. It was that his spirit was finished with this business and he now yearned for a very different life for himself and his family. He wanted to move to Ecuador and have more time to be with his wife and kids, something he did not have enough of in his present situation.

There was no logical reason for this dream. He hadn't traveled before. He had never been to Ecuador. He didn't speak a foreign language or own a passport. Yet it called to him and wouldn't leave him alone.

It seemed like a crazy idea. His business was solid and so was his income. He had all that he needed and was in complete charge of his life. His parents and siblings thought he had lost his mind and didn't support him at all. They reminded him that he had no other means of income and would put everyone at risk if he picked up and quit. They said it was selfish and stupid, and almost forbade him to go.

But the truth of the matter was that his heart and spirit had already quit and were no longer committed to the business at hand, and it showed. Profits were down, he experienced one problem after another, and his day-to-day life was joyless and frustrating.

When we spoke, he asked me if following his dream was the gross mistake everyone insisted it was and if he would later regret making the move. I was quiet for a minute and allowed his question to hang in the air like the dark, black cloud of oppression over his head that it was.

After what seemed like forever, but in truth was only 30 seconds or so, he answered his own question. "I don't know why I am asking you this question, Sonia. I know it is right for me to follow my heart and make the move to Ecuador. My wife is on board and trusts me. My kids are little and ready to go anywhere. I trust that I will be able to earn the money I need to support my family no matter where I am, because I am creative and hardworking. There are no guarantees, I know, but my heart assures me it is the right thing to do for my family and that we will be okay."

I listened. His voice was on fire with passion. He felt it too. He laughed and said, "Thank you for not answering my question. I would have still questioned myself if you had given me the answer. I needed the space to come up with the answer myself. I'm clear. I'm going to make the change."

Full of resolve, he again laughed and thanked me all over again.

Listening to his intuition and deciding that he was going to act on it openly offered him the opportunity to have a genuinely empowered, joyful, creative, dynamic, self-directed life that he would really love. All he had to do was let go of control and fear, and get into the flow of the authentic life calling to him.

The day we spoke was the day he decided he would.

I don't know what will happen to Jason and his family, but my intuition tells me that all will work out for them. I am eager to learn if it does.

CONCLUSION

Once you stop resisting the idea of following your heart rather than your head, you begin to realize that you are a super powerful spiritual being, endowed with the great and natural ability to accurately tune in to your true path. It starts when you give yourself permission to trust your intuition. No one else has the ability to do that. It comes from you because the power belongs to you.

I want to warn you, though, that there will be plenty of people who will try to discourage you from being this empowered. They might laugh at you. Roll their eyes at you. Tell you that you are crazy. Shake their heads at you. Even run from you. But they do not get to decide if you are allowed to listen to your intuition. Only you do. But along with this decision comes the need to take *100 percent responsibility* for your life. Only then can you be fully empowered.

You can no longer hope, wish, expect, or demand that someone else take care of you, no matter how much you want them to. You may be under the illusion that someone will do this for you, or should do it for you as long as you do what they want. But, in truth, that arrangement ends with childhood.

Once you become an adult, no one has to be responsible for you, or will be (unless you are an invalid, and even then you are still your own person). Taking full responsibility for your life is the single most empowering thing you can do, and the one that allows all your intuition to turn up to full volume and begin guiding you toward successfully creating the life you want to live.

In the end, allowing intuition to guide you is one of the most empowering choices you will ever make. It puts you fully in the driver's seat in your life and allows to you to take off in the direction your heart wants to go. Riding along with you will be your calm, relaxed mind and your enlivened, creative imagination. These three super powers work together to create an exciting, peaceful, and satisfying life—the life you were designed to have.

Bringing It All Together and Becoming a Super Hero in Your Own Life

A T THIS POINT, YOU MAY BE FEELING a bit overwhelmed at the prospect of incorporating all of these powerful tools for meditation, imagination, and intuition. How will you still have time in your day to do all the things you normally do?

In truth, it is far easier to make this shift into super-powered living than you might think. As a way to help you envision how this might unfold, I have created a fictional character named Sarah. Sarah is a single mother with three children, two middle schoolers and one teenager, and a career as a commercial designer for a large firm in Denver. I'm going to describe how her super-powered day unfolds as an example of how you might weave these practices into your day as well.

A Super-Powered Day

6:05 A.M. Sarah wakes up and says a quick prayer of gratitude for the blessing of awakening to another beautiful day. She sits up and moves to a chair in the corner of her bedroom, where she puts on her headphones and listens to a beautiful piece of music as she begins the Breakfast of Champions morning meditation.

6:20 A.M. Sarah gets up and stretches and heads for the shower. While in the shower she Dives for Gold, saying, "If I weren't afraid I would . . ." and fills in the blank for the next three minutes. Then she turns off the shower and begins to get dressed. Paying attention to what she said as she Dove for Gold, she decides to leave the office at 5 P.M. instead of working overtime today.

6:40 A.M. Focusing on the things she would love to create today, Sarah heads down to breakfast and mindfully starts the coffeemaker. Next she sits down, and as she waits for the coffee to brew she imagines her day ahead. She sees herself successfully closing the two projects pending on her desk, one with a very difficult client, and looks forward to the positive energy and relief that this will bring to the office all the way around.

6:50 A.M. Sarah looks at the refrigerator as she takes out the cream for her coffee and sees her list of past creations under a magnet on the refrigerator door. She says out loud, "I can't wait to put the deals I'll be closing today on this list tonight," as she shuts the refrigerator door, smiling to herself.

6:50 to 7:00 A.M. Sarah sips her coffee and breathes deeply, enjoying looking out the window.

7:00 to 7:15 A.M. Sarah prepares sack lunches for both herself and her kids.

7:15 to 7:45 A.M. Sarah wakes her kids up and gets breakfast on the table, and then hustles her kids out the door and onto the school bus.

7:45 to 8:10 A.M. Sarah clears the dishes then gets her coat and briefcase as she too heads out the door, singing "I'm a Believer" on her way to the car.

8:10 to 9:00 A.M. Sarah drives to work. As she drives she scans the traffic and checks her vibes to see if there are any traffic problems on her usual route. While not detecting traffic trouble, she does have an intuitive hit to call the office right away. Not questioning her feeling, she connects to Bluetooth and calls her boss. He informs her that it was great that she called, as the meeting they had scheduled at the office this morning has just been moved to their client's hotel instead. Thankfully, since she called when she did, she will now be able to make it on time. Sarah changes directions in the car and thanks her Higher Self for the heads-up.

9:10 A.M. Sarah arrives at the hotel and the meeting begins on time. She senses the client is not fully on board with the plans they presented, and instead of ignoring her vibes, she asks the client for feedback on what they could do to make it even better. Surprised at her perception before he even said anything, her client opens up and shares what amounts to asking for very doable changes, which they readily agree to, shaking hands and closing the deal.

10:30 A.M. Back at the office, Sarah is now working on closing the second deal. Behind her on the wall is the vision board she created with her kids last Sunday evening, displaying the vacation they all dream of taking at the end of the year.

12:20 P.M. Sarah takes a break from her project, which she is to present this afternoon, and closes her office door. She sits back to meditate and visualize her afternoon meeting. She does the "I Am Calm" meditation and ends with an affirmation that she is peaceful, calm, and grounded. Then she takes out her bag lunch, turns on some classical music on her iPhone, and relaxes as she mindfully eats her lunch.

1:00 P.M. Sarah gets ready to go to her afternoon meeting. She gathers her materials and walks mindfully to the meeting room. She is the first to arrive, so she scans the room to see how the vibes feel. She notices that the energy feels a little heavy, so she opens the door wide and blesses the room, sending it positive energy. She breathes in deeply and once again affirms that she is calm and grounded while preparing to meet her difficult client.

1:30 P.M. Sarah's client arrives along with the rest of her team. She intuitively senses tension among them, so starts to breathe calmly instead of entraining with their negative energy. She consciously remains grounded and calm and tunes in to her vibes as they sit down. She is guided to focus her calming energy toward her client and feels he just needs to be heard more than anything, so asks for his opinion first. While everyone tenses as he speaks, she listens with an open heart. She doesn't take his criticism or demands personally or allow herself to be afraid of them. At the end, she breathes deeply and thanks him for the excellent feedback, and means it. He senses her sincerity and relaxes. Everyone breathes easier. They assure her client that they can address the things he asked for immediately and agree to meet again in three days to finalize the deal. Satisfied with this, the client shakes hands with everyone and leaves. Sarah goes back to her office wondering how they are going to accomplish what they said they could do.

3:00 P.M. Instead of a coffee break, Sarah leaves her desk and goes outside and walks mindfully around the block. As she does, she notices everything around her, leaving the work problems behind for 10 minutes. She feels refreshed as she returns to complete her day.

3:20 P.M. Sarah sits at her desk quietly for three minutes and imagines that she is finishing the project easily and meeting all the new requirements her client asked for in time. She closes her eyes and immediately gets an intuitive flash to call a vendor she hasn't worked with in more than two years. She picks up the phone and dials without thinking. He answers and she asks if he can help her get the materials they need at the last minute. Laughing, he says she called in the nick of time. They just received a new shipment of product that day, and there were overages, so yes, he can get them to her right away. Hanging up she breathes a deep sigh of relief and smiles. She thanks her intuition for guiding her as she lets the people on her team know she got what they needed to complete the project on time.

5:00 P.M. Sarah closes her briefcase and heads out the door for home. She doesn't look back or hesitate and no one stops her. On the way, she imagines what she will pack for their family vacation. It's only six months away now, and she is sure they will be going.

5:40 P.M. Sarah arrives home and is greeted by her children. While they do their homework, she prepares dinner. She takes her time and doesn't rush. She mindfully stirs the water for the spaghetti and tunes in to her three kids, one at a time. Thankfully, today all seems okay.

6:30 P.M. At dinner she tells her kids about her great creation of closing one deal and solving the problem of the other and says she is going to put it on her list on the refrigerator after dinner. Then she asks each of her kids what great creation they manifested that day. They have a lively conversation as they all share their day and laugh a lot.

8:00 P.M. After dinner, Sarah sits back and enjoys her kids. They start talking about the vacation they are creating together and what each will pack. They have a lot of fun planning the great getaway. Sarah asks if any of them want to walk with her around the block before they go to bed. First one, then all three say okay. As they stroll, they each notice new things and call them out to each other, like a game.

10:00 P.M. As Sarah gets ready for bed, she says another prayer of gratitude for a successful day. She spends a moment thinking about anyone or anything she needs to forgive from that day so she can sleep in peace. Fortunately, no one comes to mind today. She congratulates herself on creating a good day and reads her book for a minute before drifting off to sleep.

I hope you can see from this that using your super powers is practical, easy, and even fun, and doesn't interrupt your day at all. Rather, introducing your super powers into your day-to-day life takes the pressure off and invites in ease and flow.

Create Your Own Super-Powered Day Jump Start . . .

As a final exercise, look over the tools and tips from all three sections and plan your own super-powered schedule for the day, just as I have with Sarah's day.

I suggest that in the beginning you don't overload your schedule. Use one or two tools or tips in the morning, one in the afternoon, and one or two in the evening for the first few days. Gradually add more until you have created the ideal super-empowered day by the end of two weeks.

You will discover that not only it is easier than you think to live a super-empowered life, it is actually fun to live this way. And it's far easier than struggling, worrying, and feeling stuck. If you make a genuine effort, you will be delighted with the results—I promise.

Once you get a feel for living a super-empowered life, you will never go back to the old way again. Trust the process and be patient, especially with your meditation practice. Note your progress in your notebook. Above all, enjoy the process and don't make this a burden but a blessing.

I am confident that soon you will be on your way to enjoying all the blessings you yearn for and deserve, and blessing the planet with your joyful and peaceful presence along the way.

All my love,
Sonia

BONUS CONTENT

Thank you for purchasing *Your 3 Best Super Powers* by Sonia Choquette. This product includes a free download! To access this bonus content, please visit www.hayhouse .com/download and enter the Product ID and Download Code as they appear below.

Product ID: 5144

Download Code: ebook

For further assistance, please contact Hay House Customer Care by phone: US (800) 654-5126 or INTL CC+(760) 431-7695 or visit www.hayhouse.com/contact.

Thank you again for your Hay House purchase. Enjoy!

Hay House, Inc. • P.O. Box 5100 • Carlsbad, CA 92018 • (800) 654-5126

Caution: This audio program features meditation/visualization exercises that render it inappropriate for use while driving or operating heavy machinery.

Publisher's note: Hay House products are intended to be powerful, inspirational, and life-changing tools for personal growth and healing. They are not intended as a substitute for medical care. Please use this audio program under the supervision of your care provider. Neither the author nor Hay House, Inc., assumes any responsibility for your improper use of this product.

ACKNOWLEDGMENTS

I WOULD LIKE TO ACKNOWLEDGE the magnificent help and support I have been given by my dear friend and masterful editor, Linda Kahn, who has worked alongside me for the last 12 years, helping me express myself in the best possible way in this and most of my past books. Thank you Linda once again for your gracious and loving assistance in shaping this book into a work I can be proud of. Without you I would be lost.

I would like to also thank my mom who is an incredible light in my life and always has been. If there was ever anyone who has demonstrated the undeniable power of love, belief, prayer, and imagination it is you. I am so grateful you taught me how to follow my heart, listen to my spirit, and fearlessly live my truth.

To my gorgeous and beloved daughters, Sonia Soraya and Sabrina Isabel, who have delighted me beyond measure from the moment you both took your first breath. You have challenged me to be the best mother and person I can be, championed me through thick and thin, forgave me for my mistakes, laughed with me until we cried, and dared to believe with me along the way. You are my best friends, and greatest treasures. Thank you for the gift of your light and love in my life.

I would also like to thank all my beautiful clients over the years. Thank you for sharing your lives, your stories, your pain, and your victories with me. You are all my true heroes and I am deeply grateful for your generosity, inspiration, and trust.

I would like to thank my lifelong friend, and gifted intuitive guide and teacher LuAnn Glatzmaier, for shining light on my path for the past 40 years. You have kept me laughing and loving, even through my darkest hours. You are one of my greatest super heroes and I am grateful for your wisdom, humor, insight, and friendship.

To my dear friend Julia Cameron, who believed in me when I didn't believe in myself. You gave me the confidence to write, which is one of the greatest blessings and joys of my life. You opened the way, Julia. I am profoundly grateful for you believing in me.

I would also like to acknowledge and thank my dear friend, business partner, and manager Ryan Kaiser. Your steady help, creativity, and flawless integrity have allowed me to relax and focus on writing, consulting, and teaching while you steer our boat. Thank you for being the best, most grounded person, and partner in the world. You are my rock and I am eternally grateful for your love, professionalism, and solid support.

I would also like to thank my dear family at Hay House. I am so blessed by your "believing eyes" and have been from the beginning of our relationship. To Louise Hay, who is our timeless and magnificent leader. To Reid Tracy, Margarete Nielsen, Michelle Pilley, Patty Gift, Sally Mason my gorgeous editor, and all the behind the scenes Hay House helpers who help bring my message to the world. I am grateful beyond words for all of you. You are a true Super Power in the world and it is an honor and privilege to be part of your brilliant light brigade. I am deeply blessed and grateful to all of you. I thank you with all my heart.

ABOUT
the
AUTHOR

S ONIA CHOQUETTE is celebrated worldwide as an author, spiritual teacher, six-sensory consultant, healer, and transformational visionary guide. An enchanting storyteller, Sonia is known for her delightful humor and adept skill in quickly shifting people out of psychological and spiritual difficulties, and into a healthier energy flow. Because of her unique gifts, Sonia's expertise is sought throughout the world, helping both individuals and organizations dramatically improve their experience and abilities to perform optimally through empowerment and transformation.

Sonia attended the University of Denver and the Sorbonne in Paris, and also holds a doctorate from the American Institute of Holistic Theology. Sonia presently lives in Paris. Website: www.soniachoquette.net.

Hay House Titles of Related Interest

YOU CAN HEAL YOUR LIFE, the movie,
starring Louise Hay & Friends
(available as a 1-DVD program and an expanded 2-DVD set)
Watch the trailer at: www.LouiseHayMovie.com

THE SHIFT, the movie, starring Dr. Wayne W. Dyer
(available as a 1-DVD program and an expanded 2-DVD set)
Watch the trailer at: www.DyerMovie.com

***

10 SECRETS FOR SUCCESS AND INNER PEACE,
by Dr. Wayne W. Dyer

THE COURAGE TO BE CREATIVE: How to Believe in Yourself,
Your Dreams and Ideas, and Your Creative Career Path,
by Doreen Virtue

MEDITATIONS TO HEAL YOUR LIFE, by Louise Hay

MEET YOUR SOUL: A Powerful Guide to Connect
with Your Most Sacred Self, by Elisa Romeo

MIRACLES NOW: 108 Life-Changing Tools for Less Stress, More
Flow, and Finding Your True Purpose, by Gabrielle Bernstein

All of the above are available at your local bookstore,
or may be ordered by contacting Hay House (see next page).

***

We hope you enjoyed this Hay House book. If you'd like to receive our online catalog featuring additional information on Hay House books and products, or if you'd like to find out more about the Hay Foundation, please contact:

Hay House, Inc., P.O. Box 5100, Carlsbad, CA 92018-5100
(760) 431-7695 or (800) 654-5126
(760) 431-6948 (fax) or (800) 650-5115 (fax)
www.hayhouse.com® • www.hayfoundation.org

* * *

Published and distributed in Australia by: Hay House Australia Pty. Ltd., 18/36 Ralph St., Alexandria NSW 2015 • *Phone:* 612-9669-4299 *Fax:* 612-9669-4144 • www.hayhouse.com.au

Published and distributed in the United Kingdom by:
Hay House UK, Ltd., Astley House, 33 Notting Hill Gate, London W11 3JQ *Phone:* 44-20-3675-2450 • *Fax:* 44-20-3675-2451 • www.hayhouse.co.uk

Published and distributed in the Republic of South Africa by:
Hay House SA (Pty), Ltd., P.O. Box 990, Witkoppen 2068
info@hayhouse.co.za

Published in India by: Hay House Publishers India, Muskaan Complex, Plot No. 3, B-2, Vasant Kunj, New Delhi 110 070 *Phone:* 91-11-4176-1620 • *Fax:* 91-11-4176-1630 • www.hayhouse.co.in

Distributed in Canada by:
Raincoast Books, 2440 Viking Way, Richmond, B.C. V6V 1N2
Phone: 1-800-663-5714 • *Fax:* 1-800-565-3770 • www.raincoast.com

* * *

Take Your Soul on a Vacation

Visit www.HealYourLife.com® to regroup, recharge, and reconnect with your own magnificence.Featuring blogs, mind-body-spirit news, and life-changing wisdom from Louise Hay and friends.

Visit www.HealYourLife.com today!